Brush-up java
for
Interview

Java concepts refresher.

(Covers up to java 11)

Ashutosh Shashi

2

Brush-up java for interview: Java concepts refresher
Copyright © 2020 by Ashutosh Shashi

ISBN 9781735222233

DEDICATION

To my parents,
Mr. Ram Binod Sharma and Mrs. Ramsukumari Devi for their blessings.
To my wife Neha for her unconditional support.
And
Thanks to my dear daughter Anvita for 'cover and more drawings' of this book.

This page is intentionally left blank

Table of Contents

6

About the Author

Ashutosh Shashi is a visionary and innovative technologist, currently living in Atlanta, Georgia, USA. He has completed master's degree in Computer Applications. He has more than 15 years of experience in IT industry. He is an architect, trainer, and author.

He is TOGAF 9.1 Certified, Google Cloud Certified Professional Cloud Architect, Microsoft Certified AZURE Solutions Architect Expert, AWS Certified Solutions Architect – Associate, Project Management Professional (PMP), DataStax Certified Professional on Apache Cassandra, and Oracle Certified Java SE 8 programmer.

One can define him as a deep reader, dedicated writer and technology passionate person. He loves to keep himself updated with the latest stack of technologies and industry standards.

Introduction

This book is useful for developers who has prior java development experience and wants to scale up or brush up their knowledge. It will be helpful for interview preparations. One can use it as a tool to crack the java interview.

This book is not in the form of interview questions and answers. It is specially designed to brush-up the java concepts quickly so that you will be capable to answer java interview questions.

This book contains small code snippet as example code. All code is tested, and you will be able to compile and run in single java file.

This book covers almost all the concepts of Java, up to java 11, that you need to know for interview.

Please send your suggestion and feedback in email at: bjava@ashutoshshashi.com

1   Basic Java Concepts

Java is a general purpose, concurrent, object-oriented programming language. Java programming language is a statically typed language, meaning, in Java every variable and every expression has a type known at compile time. Types in Java is divided in two category, Primitive Type and Reference Type.

Primitive types are reserved keyword (pre-defined in Java) that is used to define a type of a variable. Primitive types are boolean, int, long, short, float, double, byte, and char.

Reference types are referenced to the objects. Reference types are class type, interface type, array type, and type variables.

Java is platform independent, object-oriented, and multithreaded programming language. Here platform-impendent means you can write the code once and run in any platform. In other words, Java is not operating system dependent, you just need to have

JVM installed in your machine and you can run same code in any operating system. We will discuss more about JVM in a separate chapter.

Object oriented programming is a programming technique that use objects and their interfaces to build building blocks. We will discuss more about it in a separate chapter.

Multithreaded meaning Java have capability that can be used to write concurrent program and java will run it concurrently. We will discuss multithreading in a separate chapter.

Class, interface & package

Package

Package is a directory in which programs or sub packages are organized. Package is a group of classes or interfaces or both. A package can have sub package and sub package can have programs (.java files). Programs are the class and interface files. Naming structure of a package is hierarchical, and member of a package are class and interface. In java.io, java is a package and io is a sub package. You can also say java.io is a package. Package helps to prevent name conflict. Two packages in java cannot be exactly same in same hierarchy. For example, you cannot have two java.io package. Because package prevent name conflict you can have class or interface with the same name in two different packages but not in the same package. However, having class or interface with the same name is not a good practice, if you have it then you may have to use class or interface name with full package hierarchy.

```
1. package ashu.tech;
2.
3. import ashu.tech.basic.SameNameClass;
4.
5. public class MyMainClass {
6.
7.   public static void main(String[] args) {
8.
9.     SameNameClass obj1 = new SameNameClass();
10.
11.    ashu.tech.jvm.SameNameClass obj2 = new
12.            ashu.tech.jvm.SameNameClass();
13.
14.          }
15.
16. }
```

In above code snippet, I have class SameNameClass in two package, one package it is importing and another package it is providing with full qualifier path. This happens only if you have class with same name in more than one package and you are using those in one class like above.

Class

Class is a template or logical construct, on which the whole Java programming language is based upon. In java specification class is defined as a reference type and it describes how that reference type is implemented. An Object class is the parent of all the classes in Java. Every class you create in Java, or any class that exists in Java is derived from Object class.

A class can be derived from a class or interface. Once you derive the class from a class or interface, it extends the functionality of base class. Members of base class will be visible in derive class is based on the access specified you have used to define members of base class. As Object class in the base class of all the classes in Java, methods of Object class are available in every class by default. You can have your own implementation (override) of object class method to manage the behavior of your class. Object class methods are: clone(), equals(), finalize(), getclass(), hashcode(), notify(), notifyAll(), toString(), and wait(). We will talk about Object class and its methods in detail in separately.

Members of the class can be defined with public, protected, default, and private access specifiers. Below is the explanation of access specifiers.

- **public** - Members defined with public access specifier can be accessed from anywhere, inside or outside of the class.
- **protected** – Members defined with protected access specifier can be accessed from inside the class, or it can be accessed within the same package, or it can be accessed in first level derived class.
- **Default** – Members defined without any access specifier is considered as default or package-private access specifier. Exception is in interface where if you do not specify access specifier and by default it will be public. In class it will be default or package private. Default access specifier can be accessed from inside of the class and also can be accessed within the same package. Default cannot be accessed in derived class, if member of base class is default and base and derived classes are in different package. If base class and derived class are in same package, then member of base class with default access specifiers will be accessed in derived class.

- **private** – Members defined with private access specifier can be accessed only from inside the class. Then what is the use of private access specifier? You can have public member that can be called outside of class and through public member you can call or manipulate the private member of class. For example, you have private variable in a class that you do not want anyone can modify freely. You want to control the modification process of that private variable that is why you declared it as private. Now you can have public method inside the same class (for example getter and setter methods) that can be used outside of the class to access or modify the variable. You will have more control on private variable.

Member fields of class can be declared as private, unless you have any special circumstances. Class methods should have minimum accessibility, if you are calling method only inside your class, you can make it private. Always try to make each class members as less accessible as possible.

Below table will be helpful to understand the visibility of access specifiers. Below table is applicable for both instance variable and instance methods.

	Within Class	Within Package	Across Package
public	Yes	Yes	Yes
protected	Yes	Yes	No (Yes, for subclass)
default	Yes	Yes	No
private	Yes	Yes	No

In above table you can see if access specifier is protected, members will not be visible outside of package that is similar to default access specifier. But if base class is having protected member, subclass can see that protected member even though base class and subclass is from different package.

Interface

Interface is a reference type whose members are classes, interfaces, constants, and methods. While creating interface, the file name should be same as the interface name. An interface can declare one or more abstract methods. Unrelated class may implement the same interface to by providing implementation of interface methods, it allows you to implement some common behavior in both similar and unrelated class. Class can implement one or more interface, implementing interface force the class to implement all the abstract methods defined in interface.

An interface can extend another interface. When class implements interface, class has to implements all of its abstract methods plus all the abstract method in the interface extended by interface you have implemented. See the below example.

```
1. public interface LivingThings {
2.
3.   void breath();
4. }
```

LivingThings interface defined the abstract method breath(). Any class implementing this interface has to implement breath() method, or else it will result in compile time error.

```
1. public class Ladybug implements LivingThings {
2.
3.   @Override
4.   public void breath() {
5.         // TODO Auto-generated method stub
6.
7.   }
8.
9. }
```

In above example Ladybug class has implemented the interface LivingThings. Here @override annotation is optional, even though if you will not have @override annotation, it will not give you any error. You should have implementation of abstract method. It is best practice to have @override method, by using @override annotation you are announcing that this method is overridden and do not remove or modify this method, if you will modify the name of the method or arguments of the method, it will be compile time error.

Now let's see an example for interface extending another interface.

```
1. public interface Animal extends LivingThings {
2.
3.   void eatFood();
4. }
```

In above code I have defined an interface Animal that extends LivingThings interface. LivingThings is having one abstract method breath(). Animal interface has one abstract method eatFood(). Now any class that will implements Animal interface has to write implementation for both `eatFood()` and `breath()` methods, or else you will get compile-time error. In below example Elephant class is implementing Animal interface, and it has to implement both the methods.

```
1.  public class Elephant implements Animal {
2.
3.     @Override
4.     public void breath() {
5.            // TODO Auto-generated method stub
6.
7.     }
8.
9.     @Override
10.    public void eatFood() {
11.           // TODO Auto-generated method stub
12.
13.    }
14.
15.    }
```

 Question is, what the use of two separate interface is, LivingThings and Animal? Answer is interface segregation principle. Similar to the Animal interface you can have Plant interface that will extend the LivingThings interface, as below.

```
1.  public interface Plants extends LivingThings {
2.
3.     void makeFood();
4.  }
```

In above example, mock customer session Plants interface extends LivingThings. Any class that will implements Plants interface has to write implementation for both the methods defined in LivingThings and Plants.

```
1.  public class FloweringPlant implements Plants {
2.
3.     @Override
4.     public void breath() {
5.            // TODO Auto-generated method stub
6.
7.     }
8.
9.     @Override
```

```
10.  public void makeFood() {
11.          // TODO Auto-generated method stub
12.
13.  }
14.
15.  }
```

Array

Array is a data structure that can hold more than one value of same data type. Size of array should be provided at the time of creation. Arrays stores more than one value of same data type and having fix length.

Arrays are reference type objects that can be created dynamically using new operator. All elements of array will be of same type, if array is storing the element of type T then you can write array as T[], here T is also called element type of array. The element type of array can be primitive or reference type. As element type can be reference type and array itself is a reference type, an element type of array can be of array type. An element type can be abstract class type as well, and for such type null values are allowed in array.

A variable of array type holds the reference of the objects. When you create an array, it does not create an array object, and does not allocate any space for array components. It just creates a variable which can contain a reference to an array. Once array object gets created its length cannot be changed. Array can be created either by array creation expression or by an array initializer.

Array can be declared as –

```
Int [] studentId;
```

Now you create object reference with array length of size 10 as –

```
studentId = new int [10];
```

In one line it is –

```
Int [] studentId = new int [10];
```

It creates an integer array that can store 10 student IDs.

Below are the examples.

```
    int [] intArray = new int [5]; //array of int with length 5.

    Short [] productIds = new short [25]; // array of short that
can store 25 short values.
```

```
   Exception ex [] = new Exception [5]; // array of Exception
objects that can store 5 exception objects.

   Object exp [] = new Exception [5]; // array of Exceptions that
can store 5 Exception objects.

   Int [] deptNos = {101,102,103,104,105}; // creating array
using initializer.

String [] colorCds = {"GR", "BL", "RD"}; // creating array using
initializer.
```

Arrays are objects, you can assign arrays to another reference variable of Object type.

```
int [] studentId = new int [50];
Object obj = studentId;
```

In above code segment is creating an array object and assigning it to the reference variable. Here obj holds the reference of int [] studentId. Every array is an object, but every object is not an array. You can assign obj object back to the array. Like –

```
Int [] stdId = (int []) obj;
```

To cast back to appropriate array type you must have information about obj object type.

All array store values based on index, and index starts with zero. You can access value from an array based on the index, you do not have to iterate the whole array to access of a value from a particular index. But if you have an array and you need to check for some value inside this array, you don't know the index then you have to iterate array in loop. Once you store data in array, array does not change the order of data, it maintains the order. For example, if you have int array can store 10 integer value, the value stored at index zero will always be accessible from index zero, the value stored at index one will always get accessible from index one, and so on. Arrays are objects that gets created on heap not stack, every array has its size at the creation time, if you will not provide the size of an array it will be compile time error. Array index starts with zero and goes up to (length of array -1). If you have array of length 10 then your index will start from Zero and will go up to Nine. If you will try to access value from array using invalid index, it will throw the run time exception ArrayIndexOutOfBoundsException. Invalid index meaning if you are trying to access value from array using negative index or providing index that is more than the (array length -1).

You cannot change the size of array at run time. You cannot use generics in Array. You cannot pass negative number as size of array.

```
int [] arr = new int [-1]; // this will throw
java.lang.NegativeArraySizeException
```

You can pass Zero as size of array, though it is perfectly valid and not give any error, but it is useless. As length of array will be zero, and you cannot store any value in this array.

```
int [] arr = new int [0]; // this is valid
arr[0] = 5; // as size is Zero, this will throw
java.lang.ArrayIndexOutOfBoundsException
```

Any array can be assigned to the reference type, once you assigned to the Object type and try to store unrelated value then it will give you ArrayStoreException. See the below code snippet.

```
Object [] arr = new String [2]; // array of String created as
Object type.
arr [0] = "Hello"; //perfectly fine - storing String.
arr [1] = 5;// run-time exception - ArrayStoreException.
```

Here you will not get compile time exception, but you will get ArrayStoreException run time exception as you are trying to store integer into String array. You can create Object array to store any reference type as below.

```
1.          Object[] arr = new Object[2];
2.          arr [0] = "Hello";
3.          arr [1] = 5;
4.          System.out.println(arr [0]);
5.          System.out.println(arr [1]);
```

Above code is perfectly fine, and after running it will return below output.
```
Hello
5
```

Compiler checks type of the array and in case of any type mismatch it will cause compile time error. It is perfectly fine to assign array of size 4 to the array of size 2, after assigning bigger array to smaller array, you may lose data. See below example.

```
1.  Object [] arr = new Object [2];
2.
3.  Object [] arr2 = new Object [4];
4.  arr2 [0] = "hello";
5.  arr2 [1] = 5;
6.  arr2 [2] = "hi";
7.  arr2 [3] = 6;
8.
9.  arr = arr2; //assign big to small
10.
11.  System.out.println(arr [0]); // print hello
12.  System.out.println(arr [1]); // print 5
```

 If you assign big array to small, it starts copying the value and copy up to the size of destination array. Java provides Arrays class to work on array. It provides lots of utility method to make your life easy, like clone and sort. You can use Arrays.copyOf() method to copy array. It also provides Arrays.equals() method to check equality of array or Arrays.deepequals() to check equality in multi-dimensional array.

Array can be anonymous. Anonymous array is an array without having reference. You can use anonymous array inline at same place.

```
new int []{1, 2, 3, 4, 5}; // anonymous array
```

you may pass anonymous array as an argument of a method, like -

```
System.out.println(new int []{1, 2, 3}[1]); // prints 2
System.out.println(new int []{1, 2, 3}.length); // prints 3
```

Array can be defined in different styles like `int [] a` or and `int a []` both styles are valid and same thing.

Java supports n dimensional array. `int a [3][3]` is a two-dimensional array representing 3X3 matrix. `int [3][2][4]` is a three-dimensional array and so on.

If you have moved to java from c programming background, always remember that array of `char` is not `String`, and String is not an array of `char` terminated by `'\u0000'`

(NUL). A String in java is immutable whose content never change, whereas array of char has mutable elements. One has advantage over another depends where you are using it. If you are using to store password, you may choose array of char, so that you can modify same element when you change it to encrypted password. If you will String, it will create another String to store encrypted password and one can take memory dump to see both un-encrypted and encrypted password.

pass-by-value

As in java specification, java is always pass-by-value. If you worked on C++ earlier, you may confuse here. In java there is nothing called pass-by-reference.

When you are passing a value in java, it is passing a copy of value, and interestingly copy of value can make change in actual value of object. What you pass is a copy of value or reference of the same object. Here reference does not mean pass by reference. It is a reference that will point the real value in the heap. In case of primitive, that stores in stack, it preserves local value. We will see the example below.

```
1.   public static void main (String [] args) {
2.
3.        int val = 10;
4.        testMethod(val);
5.        System.out.println(val);
6.
7.   }
8.
9.   static void testMethod (int val)
10.  {
11.        val = 20;
12.  }
```

Output of this program will be 10. You have changed the value of val in method that did not reflect outside the method.

```
1. public class MyMainClass {
2.
3.   public static void main (String [] args) {
4.
5.        Student obj = new Student (10);
6.        testMethod(obj);
7.        System.out.println(obj.getId());
8.
```

```
9.    }
10.
11.  static void testMethod(Student obj)
12.    {
13.          obj.setId(20);// setting new student Id.
14.    }
15.
16.  }
17.
18.  class Student
19.  {
20.          Student(int id){
21.                this.id = id;
22.          }
23.
24.          int id;
25.
26.          public int getId() {
27.                return id;
28.          }
29.
30.          public void setId(int id) {
31.                this.id = id;
32.          }
33.
34.  }
```

Output:
20

The output of above program is 20. Here Student object is passed by value and working on the same object. The `testMethod()` modify the object as it is working on the same copy. As it is passed-by-value, you cannot change the object itself. See the below example.

```
1. public class MyMainClass {
2.
3.   public static void main(String[] args) {
4.
5.       Student obj = new Student(10);
6.       testMethod(obj);
7.       System.out.println(obj.getId());
8.
9.   }
10.
11.   static void testMethod(Student obj)
```

```
12.    {
13.        obj = new Student(20); // This will be local
14.    }
15.
16.  }
17.
18.  class Student
19.  {
20.            Student(int id){
21.                    this.id = id;
22.            }
23.
24.            int id;
25.
26.            public int getId() {
27.                    return id;
28.            }
29.
30.            public void setId(int id) {
31.                    this.id = id;
32.            }
33.
34.  }
```

Output:
10

The output of above program is 10. You can see here testMethod() is trying to update the object reference with the new address, but what testMethod() is creating is local to the method. I hope you understand the pass-by-value in Java. Let's see one more example of String. This will give you complete idea that how pass-by-value behaves on immutable class. I assume you already know the basic nature of immutable class, if you change the value of string it will create completely new object instead of changing the value in same object. Now you can guess about what will happen if you will change the value of String in testMethod(). See the example below.

```
1.    public static void main(String[] args) {
2.
3.        String str = "Hello";
4.        testMethod(str);
5.        System.out.println(str);
6.
7.    }
8.
9.    static void testMethod(String str)
```

```
10.  {
11.      str = "Hi"; // This will be local
12.  }
```

Output:
Hello

The output of above program is `Hello`. The `testMethod()` is trying to create new object, and that new object is local to the `testMethod()`. Always remember this String behavior, this is very important. String is immutable and every time you change the value, it creates new String. Be careful when you are passing String to the method.

2   JVM

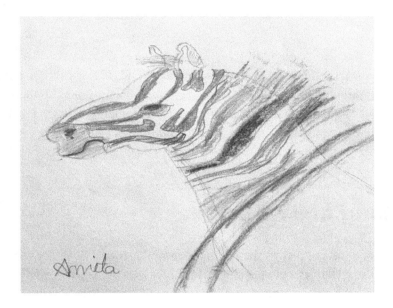

Java Virtual Machine (JVM) is an abstract computing machine, that works similar to the real computing machine. JVM contains the instruction sets, using that, it manipulates various memory areas at runtime. JVM is the part of Java Runtime Environment (JRE).

The JVM is the integral part of JRE, JVM comes with the JRE package. If you go to the JRE download page in oracle or any of the OpenJDK provider website, it will ask you to download the JRE based on your operating system. Different JRE gets downloaded for different operating systems, like LINUX, Mac, or Windows. JRE is needed on the machine of end user of your program (usually servers that will run your program), that need it to run the program, and the program will run on top of JVM that is inside JRE.

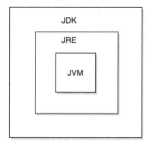

JDK is the superset that contains JVM, JRE, and JDK. JRE is runtime environment that contains JVM and the library classes to use to run java programs. JDK is Java development Kit, that contains JRE and java development kit. Java development kit provides the environment to develop the Java program. JRE executes what you developed using java development kit. In short, developers machine needs JDK and end user or servers where application runs needs JRE.

Working of JVM

Once java code is completed, the compiler compiles that code to convert the .java files to the .class files. All of the class and interface files gets converted into separate .class file, one .class file for one java class or one interface. These .class files is called bytecode. The primary Java compiler that converts human readable program (.java file) to the byte code (.class file) is javac compiler, javac compiler is included in JDK.

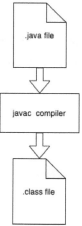

Compiled code stored in system-independent binary format known as class file format.

JVM expects that nearly all type checking is done prior to run time, typically by a compiler, and does not have to be done by JVM itself.

Run time data area

JVM defines various runtime data areas that are used during execution of program.

- **The pc (program counter) Register**: JVM supports many concurrent thread executions, each JVM has its own pc register. At any point each JVM thread is executing the code of a single method, called current method for that thread. The pc register is wide enough to store return address of that native method JVM thread is executing.

- **JVM stacks**: Each JVM thread has a private JVM stack that is created when JVM thread gets created. JVM stacks are used to hold local variables and partial results, it also does the method invocation and return. Program can have fixed size of JVM stack, or you can define JVM stacks as dynamically expendable for your program. You can define initial size of JVM stacks. In case of dynamically expanding JVM stacks, you can define minimum and maximum size of stack. If computation in JVM thread requires larger JVM stack than is permitted, the JVM throws a `StackOverflowError`. If you set JVM stack to expand dynamically, while attempting to expend the JVM stack if insufficient memory is available, JVM throws an `OutOfMemoryError`.

- **Heap**: Heap is the run-time data area that is shared among all JVM threads. Heap is created on virtual machine start-up and reclaimed by garbage collector, an automatic storage management system. The memory for heap does not need to be contiguous. You can provide initial size of heap, and minimum and maximum heap size for the auto expended heaps. If computation required more heap than it can be made available by automatic storage management system based on what values you have provided for memory, JVM throws an `OutOfMemoryError`.

- **Method Area**: The JVM has a method area that is shared among all the JVM threads. Method area is a storage area for compiled code, analogous to the text segment in operating system process. It stores each class instruction for class and interface, like run-time constant pool, field and method data, and the codes for methods and constructors. You can provide initial size, minimum, and maximum size for method area. If method area memory cannot made available on allocation request, JVM throws an `OutOfMemoryError`.

CLASS file verification

A JVM verifies that each class files to ensure that class file satisfies the necessary constraints at linking time. Class files gets generated by compiler then you may think what the use of class file verification is done by JVM. This is done because of following reasons.

- To determine that the class file is generated by trustworthy compiler. This is very important for security.
- If you have downloaded already compiled file, JVM wants to ensure that the class files are in good shape, properly formed, and properly downloaded.
- To check the binary compatibility, it verifies class file. Let's say you have compiled class file that was compiled long back with some other version.
- Verification at linking time increase performance by not doing expensive checks to verify constraints for each interpreted instruction at run-time.

JVM Startup

The JVM starts up with a sequence of operations to initialize, load, and link all the class, interface, method, operation, and so on. It takes few seconds to startup the JVM, you will see some time it takes few moments to enable your service after programs shows it is running. That is the startup time. First JVM creates initial class, which is specified in an implementation-dependent manner, using the bootstrap class loader. The JVM then links the initial class, initializes it, and invokes the `main()` method. The invocation of `main()` method drives all further execution. The `main()` method cause linking of additional classes and interfaces, as well as invocation of additional methods. You can provide initial class to JVM by command line arguments as well.

Loading

Loading is the process of finding the binary representation of a class or interface type with a particular name and creating a class or interface from that binary representation.

There are two kind of class loaders, the bootstrap class loader and user-defined class loader. Bootstrap class loader is supplied by JVM, user-defined class loader is an instance of a subclass of the abstract `ClassLoader`. User-defined class loaders can be used to create classes that originate from user-defined sources.

An array class is created directly by JVM not by class loader. The array class do not have external binary representation, they are created by JVM rather than class loader.

If an error occurred during class loading, then subclass of `LinkageError` must be thrown at a point in program that use the class or interface being loaded. Subclasses of LinkageError indicate that a class has some dependency on another class; however, the latter class has incompatibly changed after the compilation of the former class. You will see one of the exceptions that is the subclass of `LinkageError`. `BootstrapMethodError`, `ClassCircularityError`, `ClassFormatError`, `ExceptionInInitializerError`, `IncompatibleClassChangeError`, `NoClassDefFoundError`, `UnsatisfiedLinkError`, `VerifyError`.

Class loader loads class recursively to load super classes, it throws `ClassNotFoundException` if it failed to load superclass that exception is wrapped in a `NoClassDefFoundError`.

Given the same name a class loader should always return the same class object.

Linking

Linking is the process of taking a class or interface and combining into the run-time state of the JVM so that it can be executed. In the linking process it verifies and prepare class or interface. In this process every direct superclass and super interface also gets verified.

A class or interface should be loaded before the linking, so the loading and linking cannot be done together. Loading is successfully completed before it is linked. Linking is involves in allocation of new data structure. If allocation fails it may throw `OutOfMemoryError`. As I noted earlier that `OutOfMemoryError` thrown when the JVM cannot allocate an object because it is out of memory, and no more memory could be made available by the garbage collector. Linking involves the following processes.

- **Verification**: It verify if binary representation of class and interface is structurally correct. If verification of binary representation of class or interface is failed, then it throws `VerifyError`. Verification may cause additional class and interface to be loaded. JVM throws `LinkageError` or subclass of `LinkageError,` in case of failure of verification.
- **Preparation**: Preparation is creating static fields for a class or interface and initializing such fields to their default values.
- **Resolution**: Resolution dynamically determine concrete values from symbolic references in the run-time constant pool. All references to the variable and methods are stored in the class's constant pool as a symbolic reference. A symbolic reference is a logical reference not a reference that actually points to a

physical memory location. For example, `instanceof`, that is the JVM instruction make symbolic reference to the runtime constant pool. It is used to determine if object is of given type. Resolution also does field lookup, method resolution, interface method resolution, access control, and overriding.

Initialization

Initialization of a class or interface is to executing initialization method of class or interface. A class or interface should be verified and prepared before initialization. The referenced class or interface is initialized on execution of `new` instruction from JVM, if it is not already initialized. The class or interface will be initialized on execution of `getstatic`, `putstatic`, or `invokestatic` JVM instructions. Class or interface can also be initialized on invocation of reflective method in the class library, or initialization of one of the subclasses. As JVM is multithreaded, multiple thread may try to initialize the same class or interface at the same time, it requires careful synchronization of class and interface because of this multithreaded nature.

Binding

Binding is the process that is completely different than linking, through which functions written in other language integrated with the JVM so that it can be executed.

JVM EXIT

JVM exits when any thread invokes the `exit` method of `Runtime` or `System` class. JVM can also be exited with the `halt` method of `Runtime` class. `Exit` or `Halt` operation must be permitted by the security manager.

JIT Compiler

JIT is Just-in-time compiler that do the performance optimization at run-time. JIT compiler is the essential part of JRE. JIT compilers interacts with the JVM at run time and compile bytecode sequence into the native machine language. JVM do not have to interpret the bytecode sequence repeatedly, instead native machine directly executes the native machine language, that improve performance and increase execution speed.

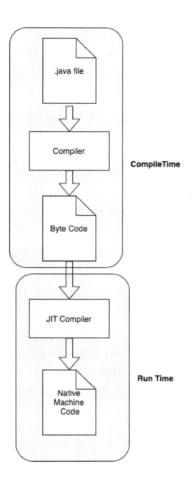

Garbage Collection

Garbage collector (GC) is a feature of Java use to deallocate or free the memory if object is no longer have any reference. If you have worked on C++, you might know, how difficult is allocating and deallocating memory, you use to implement reference counting mechanism to count the object created and deleted by your program. You need to keep track of the object and you have to remember to delete the object created once you are done with the object, otherwise memory leaks will occur and after some time the program may crash because of out of memory error.

Java solved this problem by using garbage collector (GC) algorithm. Garbage collector automatically track your object and check if your object is no longer in use JVM freed the memory occupied by that object and make that available for new objects. There is multiple GC algorithm available, you can choose the GC algorithm best suited to your application. Multiple threads of JVM works in your system, GC also runs in multiple threads, based on the chosen algorithm JVM scans heap area, find the unused object and freed them, different GC algorithm works differently.

Generation

Garbage collectors works by splitting the heap into generations. The heap is divided into two generations, `old generation` and `young generation`. `Young generation` is again divided into two parts, called `eden` and `survivor` spaces.

Young generation is a portion of heap where JVM frequently do the find and sweep operation. Once you created new object it gets allocated to the `eden` section of `young generation`. Once `young generation` is cleared during garbage collection, all objects in `eden` is either moved to `survivor` or deleted. In the same process objects from `survivor` space is moved to `old generation` or deleted. In this process `eden` and one of the `survivor` spaces is empty. Now you are wondering about one of the survivor spaces, there are more than one survivor space that is used by GC algorithm for swapping of object between different heap sections of the survivor space. During garbage collection in young generation JVM pause for a very small time for clearing all the objects called stop-the-world pause.

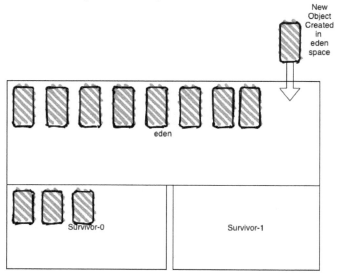

Fig: new object created in eden space of young generation

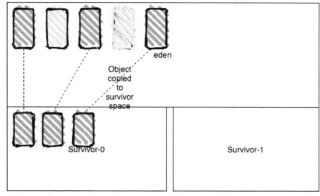

Fig: referenced object moved to survivor space and unreferenced deleted.

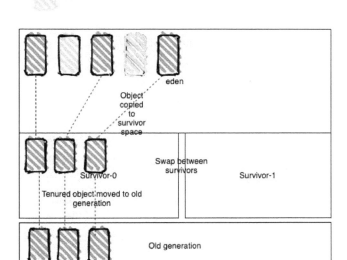

Fig: Object swapped between survivor's multiple times; tenured objects are finally moved to old generation.

When all the survivor objects moved to the old generation, old generation also gets filled and that requires garbage collected. When JVM knows that it is the time to clean up the old generation, it scans the old generation, finds the objects that are not being used, discard them, free their memory and compact the heap. This process takes little longer than the clearing the young generation (stop-the-world pause), and this process is called full GC. Here choosing the GC algorithm makes bigger impact on the full GC situation. You need to optimize the full GC situation first before the stop-the-world situation.

GC algorithm

Below is the available GC algorithm.

- **Serial GC**: This is the simplest form of garbage collector. With this GC, both minor and major GC are done serially. This is mostly used in client-side application. If you do not have low pause time requirement, this GC is best for you. If a greater number of JVM is running on the same machine than the processor, serial GC will work well. This is the top choice of virtual machine and docker container. To enable serial GC you can use command, `-XX:+UseSerialGC`.

- **The parallel GC**: The parallel garbage collector is also called throughput GC. This GC use your multiple thread to perform young generation garbage collection. If you have x number of CPUs, it uses x GC threads for GC. In JDK 8, This is the default GC for any 64-bit machine with two or more CPUs. This is useful for batch processing applications or application required more performance and long pauses are acceptable. To enable parallel GC you can use the command, `XX:+UseParallelGC`. In this GC, number of garbage collector threads can be controlled with command line options: `-XX:ParallelGCThreads=<desired number>`.

- **The CMS GC**: The Concurrent Mark Sweep (CMS) garbage collector is also known as concurrent low pause garbage collector. This is once the popular GC, is being deprecated in Java 11 and beyond, so the use of this GC is discouraged in Java 8 as well. CMS GC use the same parallel GC algorithm for the garbage collection work in young generation (minor GC). It attempts to minimize the pauses due to garbage collection by doing most of the garbage collection work concurrently with the application threads. CMS GC does garbage collection without moving the live objects and does not copy or compact the live objects. If fragmentation become problem, then allocates the larger heap. Do not use CMS garbage collector for your application as it is not recommended with the newer version of Java. You can enable CMS GC by using the command line, `-XX:+UseConcMarkSweepGC`. You can also provide the number of GC thread you want to use with CMS GC while enabling it with command line, `-XX:ParallelCMSThreads=<n>`.

- **The G1 GC**: The Garbage First (G1) garbage collector was designed for the long-term replacement of the CMS garbage collector. From Java 11 onwards, on 64-bit JVM, if machine is having more than one CPUs, G1 GC is the default garbage collector. It works well in Java 8 as well, so you can use this GC in Java 8 onwards. This garbage collector is parallel, concurrent, and low pause GC. This GC is very different layout from another GC. This GC also believe in generation and deal the young generation almost similarly as the parallel GC, but it handles old generation little differently. It divides old generation in the same way all GC divides the survivor space. It divides old generation in two parts and swaps the objects while doing garbage collection in old generation (during major GC). To enable G1 GC use command, `-XX:+UseG1GC`.

There are few command lines options you should aware of that you can use in VM arguments. It will help you to manage heap memory size and set the size for GC.

- To sets the initial heap size for when the JVM starts, use command line, `-Xms`.
- To sets the maximum heap size, use the command line, `-Xmx`.
- To sets the size of the Young Generation, use the command line, `-Xmn`.
- To sets the starting size of the Permanent Generation, use the command line, `-XX:PermSize`.
- To sets the maximum size of the Permanent Generation, use the command line, `-XX:MaxPermSize`.

3   OOP Concepts

The Object-Oriented Programming (OOP) concepts are being used since very long time and for many programing languages. OOP is a concept, programming language is based upon, it is not the technology. The key difference between technology and concepts is technology change frequently and concepts keep evolving. Java is an object-oriented language that follows classical object-oriented concepts like, abstraction, encapsulation, inheritance, and polymorphism. These four basic concepts are called four pillars of OOP programming in Java.

Classes and Objects are basics of Object-Oriented Programming (OOP). Everything in Java is defined by classes and objects. Class is a template or blueprint from which objects are created. Objects are the instance of class. Class defines set of properties and methods that are common in all the objects. The run-time behavior of object is defined by its class definition. Two instances of same class are not same, and they may contain different value, different state, and can behave differently based on class implementation. All instance method only be called by the instance of that class, but all the static method can be called directly using class name, without using an instance. When you create instance, appropriate constructor method of that class will be called.

Every object can have different data stored in the properties defined in the class. Properties are the member variable a class can be defined. A common place where you initialized or assign values to those properties is a constructor. Each object maintains different state with the different data.

Each object can have different behavior defined in the class methods. Fields in objects that is defined by class is called state of object, methods that object can call and is defined in class determines the behavior of object. Object behavior can also be defined using inheritance and polymorphism, that we will discuss here.

Abstraction

Abstraction is the process of considering something independently of its attributes and implementation. When you are using some functionality, you just use it without knowing what is happening inside. Abstraction shows only essential attributes and hides the unnecessary information to reduce complexity.

One thought is encapsulation is also a form of abstraction, it is true at some extend as you are hiding the fields and allowing to manipulate the fields using wrapping method but is a completely different concept than abstraction. In a class you defined private fields with public setter and getter method, and you allow any manipulation through the methods only. This is not abstraction, but let's say in getter or setter method you are doing lots of things, some complex calculation that caller don't need to know. Here you are abstracting the complexity. Abstraction solves the issue at design level, but encapsulation solves it at implementation level. One example is weather API, weather service providers expose weather API that will provide you weather information for your location. You just integrated weather API with your code to get the weather information, your code calls the weather API by passing the location information and display the result for users. You don't know how that weather API works, and how weather API fetch and manipulate data from satellite. So, you can say weather API abstracted all the complexity from you and you do not need to know those complexity to use weather API, this is called abstraction.

Abstract Class and method

Abstract class is a class that is declared abstract. Abstract class may include abstract method. You cannot instantiate abstract class. You can create subclass from abstract class.

Abstraction can be achieved by using abstract class and method. Class implemented abstract class will have implementation details, you can just call the method defined without knowing how it is implemented. An abstract class can have both abstract and non-abstract method. As java class does not support multiple inheritance, abstract class does not support this.

You can use abstract class and abstract method to implement abstraction.

```
1. public abstract class Shape {
2.
3.    abstract void draw();
4.
5. }
```

Shape is an abstract class that has abstract method draw(). Class Circle and Square are the subclass of the Shape abstract class. Both Circle and Square class has to implement draw() method.

Class Circle:

```
1. public class Circle extends Shape {
2.
3.    @Override
4.    void draw() {
5.          System.out.println("I am circle");
6.    }
7.
8. }
```

Class Square:

```
1. public class Square extends Shape {
2.
3.    @Override
4.    void draw() {
5.          System.out.println("I am Square");
6.    }
```

```
7. }
```

Client code:

```
1. public class MyMain {
2.
3.   public static void main(String[] args) {
4.          Shape shape = new Circle();
5.          drawShape(shape);
6.
7.          shape = new Square();
8.          drawShape(shape);
9.   }
10.
11.         public static void drawShape(Shape shape)
12.         {
13.             shape.draw(); //draw based on object type
14.         }
15.
16.   }
```

Output:
```
I am circle
I am Square
```

Here method drawShape() don't know which subclass method is being called. It is based on the object type passed to this method. Here you hide the different implementation of draw(). For client, draw is a Shape method that it can call on Circle and Square type Share object.

Interface

An interface can also be used for the abstracting. In java interface is more widely used than the abstract class. However, you can do the same thing with interface, still there are difference between interface and abstract class.

Interface	Abstract Class
Interface can have only abstract method. Since Java 8, it can have default method as well.	Abstract class can have both abstract and non-abstract method. (Almost similar since Java 8)
Interface supports multiple inheritance.	Abstract class does not support multiple inheritance.
Interface cannot provide implementation of abstract class or interface.	Abstract class can provide implementation of the interface.
Interface can only have public abstract and default methods.	Abstract class can have protected, and public abstract method.
Interface can only have public static final field.	Abstract class can have final, static, or static final fields with any access specifier.
Interface is useful for unrelated classes as well.	Abstract class is used for related classes only.

Similar to the Abstract class example below is the example for interface. Similar to the Shape abstract class, I have defined IShape interface.

```
1. public interface IShape {
2.
3.    void draw();
4. }
```

Now Circle class is implementing IShape interface, and implements draw().

```
1. public class Circle implements IShape {
2.
3.    @Override
4.    public void draw() {
5.          System.out.println("I am circle");
6.
7.    }
8. }
```

Square class is also implementing the IShape interface, and provide implementation of draw() method.

In client where the draw() method is being called.

```
1. public class MyMain {
2.
3.   public static void main(String[] args) {
4.         IShape shape = new Circle();
5.         drawShape(shape);
6.
7.         shape = new Square();
8.         drawShape(shape);
9.   }
10.
11.        public static void drawShape(IShape shape)
12.        {
13.              shape.draw();
14.        }
15.
16.  }
```

Output:
```
I am circle
I am Square
```

Here method `drawShape()` does not know the `draw()` method is being called on which object. It is based on the run-time type of the `Shape` object.

Encapsulation

Encapsulation is wrapping the data with the method. The main purpose of encapsulation is data hiding. The key difference between encapsulation and abstraction is, abstraction is used to hide the complexity or complex implementation of the functionality. In other hand encapsulation is used for data hiding. Data hiding means you are not allowing someone to manipulate or access your data directly. Using encapsulation, you can keep control of your data.

The best example of encapsulation is setters and getters in POJO classes. Whenever you create plain java class with private variables with public setter and getter methods, you are restricting users of that class to access your variable directly. As your variable is private, it can be accessed using public setters and getters method only. Below is the example of Employee class.

```
1.  public class Employee {
2.
3.      private String employeeName;
4.      private Integer employeeId;
5.      private String firstName;
6.      private String lastName;
7.      private String employeeGrade;
8.
9.      public String getEmployeeName() {
10.                 return employeeName;
11.         }
12.     public void setEmployeeName(String employeeName) {
13.                 this.employeeName = employeeName;
14.         }
15.     public Integer getEmployeeId() {
16.                 return employeeId;
17.         }
18.     public void setEmployeeId(Integer employeeId) {
19.                 this.employeeId = employeeId;
20.         }
21.     public String getFirstName() {
22.                 return firstName;
23.         }
24.     public void setFirstName(String firstName) {
25.                 this.firstName = firstName;
26.         }
27.     public String getLastName() {
28.                 return lastName;
29.         }
30.     public void setLastName(String lastName) {
31.                 this.lastName = lastName;
32.         }
33.     public String getEmployeeGrade() {
34.                 return employeeGrade;
35.         }
36.     public void setEmployeeGrade(String employeeGrade) {
37.                 this.employeeGrade = employeeGrade;
38.         }
39. }
```

All the variable in Employee class is private, if you want to access or manipulate any value, you have to go through the setter and getter method.

Now, let's say you have got the new change in above Employee class that any employee Id that is less than 100, is higher executing, and no one should be able to change the grade of those employee. You can do it very easily, because employee grade is not directly accessible and cannot be manipulated directly, you can put a condition is setter method. That's it!

```
1.    public void setEmployeeGrade(String employeeGrade) {
2.      if(employeeId <100) {
3.         System.out.println("You cannot change executives'
      grade.");
4.
5.      }else {
6.              this.employeeGrade = employeeGrade;
7.          }
8.
9.    }
```

Now no one can modify the employee grade for employee Id less than 100.

Inheritance

Inheritance is about inheriting base class features into derived class. If class A extends class B, then class A is called superclass and class B is called subclass. Subclass inherits properties and method from superclass.

Inheritance is about inheriting base class features into derived class. If class A extends class B, then class A is called superclass and class B is called subclass. Subclass inherits all the members of superclass.

Subclass cannot access superclass members that is defined as private. Private members are private to the class and it cannot be accessed outside the class including subclass.

Why Inheritance

Inheritance gives you advantage of object-oriented design. You can have base class as more generic class, in later time more class can be created using your base class. For example, you have crated base class as Animal.

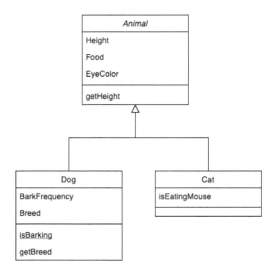

Dog and Cat class is derived from animal class. If you will not design inheritance here, Dog and Cat class should also have all the members that Animal class is having. This will increase redundancy. Another issue is consistency, you may forget to add some member in Dog class and may forgot to have member in Cat class. But in inheritance, you are explicitly providing all the required Animal member to Dog and Cat class by creating Animal base class with all the common members. Tomorrow you may need more Animal subclasses, like Tiger class, Elephant class, it will be easy to create those class by deriving those class from Animal class. Creating Animal base class can define the relationship like Dog **is-a** Animal, Cat **is-a** Animal, Tiger **is-a** Animal, and Elephant **is-a** Animal.

Inheritance defines **is-a** relationship. You create base class or superclass that is more generic and then you can create more specialized classes as subclass, that subclass will have all the members of base class plus their own members. For example, Dog is-a Animal, Dog will have all the properties of Animal plus its own special properties.

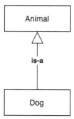

Access specifiers

- Private members are private to the class and will not get inherited to the derived class.
- Protected members of base class will get inherited in derive class. If there are multi-level inheritance, then private members are inherited to only one level of inheritance.
- Default members of base class can be inherited to the derived class if base class and derive class is in same package.
- Public members of base class always get inherited to the derived class.

Single Inheritance

Inheritance with just one base class and just one derived class is called single inheritance.

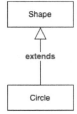

```
1. public class Shape {
2.
3.    public Integer shapeType;
4.
5.    public void draw() {
6.            System.out.println("I am Shape");
7.    }
8.
9. }
```

```
1. public class Circle extends Shape {
2.
3.
4. }
```

Here Circle class is being derived from Shape class. Here shapeType variable and draw method is available in Circle as it is defined as public.

Hierarchical Inheritance

If you are using one base class to derive multiple derived class is known as hierarchical interface.

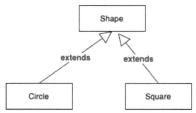

Multi-level Inheritance

Multi-level inheritance is multiple level of single inheritance. In multi-level inheritance derived class derived from base class, and then one another level of class that will get derived from derived class.

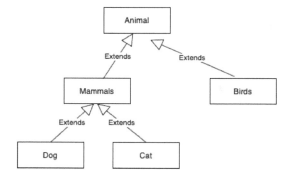

In above example, you can see Animal class is the base class for Mammals class, and again Mammals class is base class for Dog and Cat class. There is two level in this inheritance. If you have two or more level of inheritance is called multi-level inheritance.

Multiple Inheritance

Multiple inheritance is one where you can derive a class from more than one class. Java class does not support multiple inheritance, but you can implement multiple inheritance by implementing the interface.

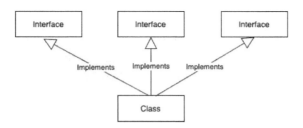

As in picture above, Java allowed to implement multiple interface for a class, that is the way you have multiple interface in Java. You can use multiple interface extended by a single class.

However, Java always extends Object class for all the classes by default and Object class members are available to use in any class you create in Java. In that way you can argue that Java allow to extend up to two class, one is Object class that is already included even if you will not extend it. If you extend super class, your class will extend actually two class, one is Object class and one is the super class that you are extending. You can argue that Java allow multiple inheritance for up to 2 class limits. But this is just an argument, you can have logically. As per Java documentation Java does not support Multiple Inheritance.

Diamond Problem

Diamond problem was C++ problem as C++ supports multiple inheritance. In java even though you can use interface to implement multiple inheritance, Interface does have only definition and classes have implementation. So, diamond problem does not occur. But since Java 8, you can have default method in interface, because of this default method diamond problem can occur in Java.

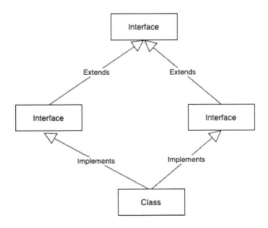

Diamond problem is actually a ambiguity, that gets created for most derived class to which version of method to use. If top level interface is having default method that is overridden in next level. The most derived class will inherit that method in two version as there is two data flow created. One version will come though left most side of interface to the class, another version of method will come though right most side of interface. This ambiguity is called diamond problem.

Composition

Composition is different than inheritance. Inheritance is defined as **is-a** relationship, but composition is defined as **has-a** relationship.

Composition is like ingredient of a food product. If you buy any food product or you make any food product you are using different ingredient to make that finished food product. You can say cake has egg in its ingredient, you can say cake is inherited from egg or egg is inherited from cake.

Let's take another example. A person has his address where he lives, he mentions his address everywhere in his identification, like driver's license, his passport, and so on. You can say a person **has-a** address. If you have a person class and a address class, person class can have address class in it to complete person class. You cannot say person is derived from address or address is derived from person. It is composition, person has address as its composition.

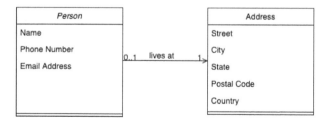

Class Address:

```
1.  public class Address {
2.
3.      private String street;
4.      private String city;
5.      private String state;
6.      private Integer postalCode;
7.      private String country;
```

```
8.
9.    public String getStreet() {
10.               return street;
11.          }
12.   public void setStreet(String street) {
13.               this.street = street;
14.          }
15.   public String getCity() {
16.               return city;
17.          }
18.   public void setCity(String city) {
19.               this.city = city;
20.          }
21.   public String getState() {
22.               return state;
23.          }
24.   public void setState(String state) {
25.               this.state = state;
26.          }
27.   public Integer getPostalCode() {
28.               return postalCode;
29.          }
30.   public void setPostalCode(Integer postalCode) {
31.               this.postalCode = postalCode;
32.          }
33.   public String getCountry() {
34.               return country;
35.          }
36.   public void setCountry(String country) {
37.               this.country = country;
38.          }
39. }
```

Class Person:

```
1. public class Person {
2.
3.    private String name;
4.    private Integer phoneNumber;
5.    private String emailAddress;
6.
7.    private Address address; //composition
8.
9.    public String getName() {
10.               return name;
11.          }
12.   public void setName(String name) {
```

48

```
13.                    this.name = name;
14.            }
15.    public Integer getPhoneNumber() {
16.                    return phoneNumber;
17.            }
18.    public void setPhoneNumber(Integer phoneNumber) {
19.                    this.phoneNumber = phoneNumber;
20.            }
21.    public String getEmailAddress() {
22.                    return emailAddress;
23.            }
24.    public void setEmailAddress(String emailAddress) {
25.                    this.emailAddress = emailAddress;
26.            }
27.    public Address getAddress() {
28.                    return address;
29.            }
30.    public void setAddress(Address address) {
31.                    this.address = address;
32.            }
33.    }
```

Above is the example of composition where Person class **has-a** address class.

Polymorphism

Polymorphism is the OOP concept that makes your program more dynamic. Polymorphism means one name with many forms. One name meaning one operation or one method and do many things. For example, + operator can be used for adding two numeric values as well as concatenation of two strings.

In java, polymorphism is a concept of binding the method with object. This binding depends on the type of object and the method parameter. Here type of object and method parameter both are very important but binding of method is more important. There can be two type of polymorphism, compile-time polymorphism and run-time polymorphism.

Compile-time polymorphism

Compile time polymorphism is the type of polymorphism where object binding with method happens at compile time. How object decides which method to call, it decides based on the parameter or arguments of the method.

Always remember that when you are talking about compile-time polymorphism you are talking about one class only. You are not talking about inheritance. Compile-time polymorphism is also called function **overloading**. Concentrate on over-**load**ing word, do not confuse with the word overriding (over-riding), over-riding is for run-time polymorphism.

Function overloading is over-load the method in the same class. Over-load meaning you have more than one method with the same name but different argument in same class.

```
1. public class OverloadingExample {
2.
3.    public void add(Integer x, Integer y) {
4.            //adding integer
5.            System.out.println(x+y);
6.    }
7.
8.    public void add(String x, String y) {
9.            //strings concatenation
10.                   System.out.println(x+y);
11.            }
12.
13.  }
```

In above example the method add() is being overloaded. Both version of method add() is in same class. If you will call add() with Integer then it will called the method with Integer arguments, if you call this method with String it will get called with String argument.

```
1.    public static void main(String[] args) {
2.      OverloadingExample obj = new OverloadingExample();
3.      obj.add(5, 6); // call method add(Integer x, Integer y)
4.      obj.add("5", "6"); // call method add(String x, String
   y)
5.    }
```

Output:
11
56

Appropriate method is getting called based on the argument. It is based on type of argument or the number of arguments. Method overloading is never depending on the return type. Return type is not get considered in method overloading. Here is another example with number of arguments.

```
1.    public void display(Integer x) {
2.        System.out.println("Displaying "+x);
3.    }
4.
5.    public void display(Integer x, Integer y) {
6.        System.out.println("Displaying "+x + "and "+y);
7.    }
```

Above is two method named display() in the same class with different number of argument. Here if you will call display() method with one integer argument then first method will get called and if you will call with two argument the second display() method will get called.

As you can overload methods in a class, you can overload constructor as well. Constructor is also a method and you can have multiple overloaded constructor.

```
1. public class OverloadingExample {
2.
3.    private int value;
4.    private String name;
5.
6.    public OverloadingExample(int value) {
7.            super();
8.            this.value = value;
9.    }
10.
11.    public OverloadingExample(int value, String name) {
12.            super();
13.            this.value = value;
14.            this.name = name;
15.            }
16.
17.    public OverloadingExample() {
18.            super();
19.            System.out.println("I am default constructor");
20.            }
21.
22.    }
```

In above code snippet, there are three overloaded constructors, one is default with no argument, one is one argument constructor and one is two argument constructors. These constructor gets called on creating objects, depends on how you are creating object, respecting constructor will get called. See below example how you can create object in three different way as you have three overloaded constructors.

```
1.   //this will call default argument (no argument)
     constructor
2.    OverloadingExample obj1 = new OverloadingExample();
3.
4.   //this will call one argument constructor
5.   OverloadingExample obj2 = new OverloadingExample(5);
6.
7.   //this will call one argument constructor
8.   OverloadingExample obj3 = new OverloadingExample(5,
     "cat");
```

In above code snippet, while creating obj1, default constructor will get called. While creating obj2, and obj3, one and two argument constructors will get called.

Run-time polymorphism

Run-time polymorphism is binding method with object at run time. This is also called method overriding. Here method name and its argument must be same in base and derived class. You might have used @override annotation while overloading of the method. If you have same method defined in base class, abstract class, or in the interface, derived class or interface implementor class will override that method. @override annotation is optional, but by putting this annotation you are documenting that you are overriding, and someone will not try to modify the method name or argument. If someone will modify method name or argument it will give compile time error. If you will not use @override annotation and you are overriding method from base class, someone can modify the method name or argument or both without getting compile time errors.

Always remember that when you are talking about run-time polymorphism or method overriding it is the same thing. Method overriding happens in inheritance, it cannot be within the same class. Method overriding always depends on the type of object at run-time, considering base class and derived class method name, number and type of argument, and return-type is same. You can see the difference that in overloading return type does not matter, but in overriding return type does matter.

Key benefit of method overriding is if you have method defined in base class, derive class can overload that method to have their own implementation or derive class can use the base class method.

Base Class:

```
1. public class BaseClass {
2.
3.    public void draw() {
4.            System.out.println("Drawing in base class");
5.    }
6.
7. }
```

Derived Class:

```
1. public class DerivedClass extends BaseClass{
2.
3. }
```

In main method:

```
1. public static void main(String[] args) {
2.          BaseClass bc = new BaseClass();
3.          bc.draw(); // call base class draw method
4.          bc = new DerivedClass();
5.          bc.draw(); // call base class draw method
6.
7.    }
```

Output:
```
Drawing in base class
Drawing in base class
```

Here whether draw method is being called using base class type of object or derived class type of object, it always calls base class method. As per inheritance rule, all public member of base class will be available for derived class. Now I changed the derived class. I am putting all code once again with changed derived class code.

Base Class:

```
1. public class BaseClass {
2.
3.    public void draw() {
4.            System.out.println("Drawing in base class");
5.    }
```

```
6.
7. }
```

Derived Class:

```
1. public class DerivedClass extends BaseClass{
2.
3.    @Override
4.    public void draw() {
5.            System.out.println("Drawing in derived class");
6.    }
7. }
```

In Main Method:

```
1.    public static void main(String[] args) {
2.            BaseClass bc = new BaseClass();
3.            bc.draw(); // call base class draw method
4.            bc = new DerivedClass();
5.            bc.draw(); // call derived class draw method
6.
7.    }
```

Output:
```
Drawing in base class
Drawing in derived class
```

 You can see that all code is same, I just added same method in derived class. See the output, now derived call type object is calling derived class method. As per inheritance rule public member of base class is still getting available, but because derived class is having the same method it is getting overridden on base class method. Here @override annotation is option, it is best practice to have this annotation.

When you are creating object like –

```
BaseClass dc = new DerivedClass();
```

Your base class object is actually pointing to derived class at run time. That is why it is calling derived class method. When base class object is pointing to the derived class object is called **upcasting**. When you do the reverse, it is called **down casting**. Below is the example. Down casting is very error prone as you are casting bigger object to the smaller object, it is not a best practice to use downcasting. Downcasting may result in ClassCastException, if not properly casted.

In C++ and C#, you declare virtual method for overriding. In java it works like virtual method in C++ or C#.

Final Keyword

If you want any method from base class should not be inherited in derived class, then you can declare that method as final method. The method declared as final in base class will not be available in derived class.

If you don't want someone extend class from your class, then you can make your class as final class. You cannot derive any class from final class.

Concept of final variable is slightly different; you must initialize the variable while declaring otherwise you will get compilation error. One other option is, you can define final variable without initializing and then initialize it in constructor. See example below.

Final method:

```
1.    public final void DefaultBehaviour() {
2.          System.out.println("I can not be inherited in
    derived class");
3.    }
```

Final Class:

```
1. public final class BaseClass {
2.
3.    public void draw() {
4.          System.out.println("You can not derive any class
    from this base class");
5.    }
6.
7. }
```

Final variable:

```
1. public class FinalTest {
2.
3.    final int count=10;
```

```
4.
5.    final int value; // compilation error
6.
7. }
```

In above code snippet, the variable count is initialized at the time when it is defined, but the variable value is not initialized and will cause compilation error.

```
1. public class FinalTest {
2.
3.    final int count=10;
4.
5.    final int value;
6.
7.    public FinalTest() {
8.        this.value = 0; // initialized in constructor
9.    }
10. }
```

Above code is perfectly fine, final variable is initialized at the same place it is defined and final variable value is initialized in constructor. This is the two way you can initialize the final variable and you should always initialize using either way or else it will give compilation error.

SOLID principle

SOLID principle is core of object-oriented design. SOLID principle defines five principle to design better software. Those five SOLID principles are.

1. **S**ingle responsibility principle.
2. **O**pen/Close principle.
3. **L**iskov Substitution Principle.
4. **I**nterface Segregation Principle.
5. **D**ependency Inversion Principle.

The SOLID principle was introduced by Robert C. Martin. Using SOLID principle, you can improve code quality. You will get less defects and maintenance of code, or enhancement of code become easy. Let's understand these five principles.

Single responsibility principle

This principle states that the class should have only one reason to change. This means the class should have only one job to do. One class should server only one purpose. All methods and properties of class should work towards the same goal. If your class is serving more than one responsibility, then you may need more than one class or separate class for the separate responsibility.

For example, if your class is parsing JSON or XML, working on business logic, and also storing and retrieving from database, then you are doing lots of work in same class. Move your database operation to the persistence layer in separate classes. Move your schema work to the model layer in separate class. Look at your business logic to make sure your class is serving just one purpose.

The more responsibility your class will handle, more often you need to change it, and your class will no longer independent from other classes. In that case changing in your class will need to change in several other classes too. Side effect of this is, your change will become more complicated than it actually is. If you follow single responsibility principle, your code will less complex, easy to understand, easy to fix any defect, easy to maintain, and less error prone.

Open/Close principle

Open/Close principle states that software entities, like your class, object, function, or module should be open for extension but closed for modification. This is the most important SOLID principle.

Following this principle, you will be able to extend the functionality of your class without modifying actual class, that is less error prone and does not impact or break existing functionality.

In the earlier example I have created Shape abstract class having *draw* method. I can say Shape class is closed now. If you need some other functionality like calculate area, you can extend another class from Shape class.

Open/Close principle is fairly simple, if your class is having some functionality and you need to implement the similar functionality to the other class, best way to extract your function to the Interface and implement that interface to those classes required that function. If you need some other function you can have some other interface from the earlier interface and implement the new interface.

Liskov Substitution principle

Liskov substitution principle talks about the ability of substitution of base class object with the derive class object. The Liskov Substitution principle was introduced by Barbara Liskov. She explained this principle as:

"Let φ(x) be a property provable about objects x of type T. Then φ(y) should be true for objects y of type S where S is a subtype of T.".

That means you should be able to replace any base class object with one of its subclass objects. If base class is doing something, derived class should be able to do the same thing.

In the earlier example I putted Shape class as base class and Circle and Square classes as derived class. If there is a method excepting the Shape object as its argument, you can use the same method to be called using Circle or Square object. You are easily substituting Circle or Square object in place of Shape object, that is called the Liskov substitution principle. You substitute with the appropriate derive class object to implement the behavior as needed.

Interface segregation principle

Interface segregation principle states that, *"A client should not be forced to implement an interface that it doesn't use."* Similar to the single responsibility principle, this principle is talking about interface. Interface should be small enough, and each interface should have related method.

If your interface is having many methods and there are many classes that is implementing your interface. Some class is implementing all the method and some class is doing false implementation by putting just placeholder, because some class does not need all the method. This is bad design as per this principle.

As class can implement multiple interface, your interface should be small enough so that it will not force any class to implement those method that it does not want. It is always better to create many small interfaces.

Dependency inversion principle

Dependency inversion principle is having two part as-

- High-level modules should not depend on low-level modules. Both should depend on abstractions.
- Abstraction should not depend on details. Details should depend on abstractions.

High level modules should not depend on low level module, both should depend on the abstraction. You can have one abstraction layer on top of both the module. By doing that your high-level and low-level module will be independent to each other.

When you are talking about abstraction, it should just define the things not implement. For example, in case of abstraction layer that is interface, interface just provides the definition and class that use those interfaces is responsible for its own implementation.

4 Class, method and Objects

Class and Object is the core of java programming. I have defined class and object multiple times in this book. Let's define it once again. Class is a template or prototype having fields and methods, and object is the instance of class. As you already know that class can have relationship with other class, it can be is-a relationship or has-a relationship. We will see more interesting facts about class and object in this chapter.

Abstract Class

I already explained about abstract class in previous chapter. Abstraction classes are needed for abstraction. Abstract class can have abstract and non-abstract method both. Abstract method should be just declaring in abstract class and non-abstract derived class should write the implementation of the abstract method. Abstract class can be inherited from another abstract class. The non-abstract class that is extending the abstract class and implement all the abstract method is called concrete class.

Final class

A class is declared as final if you do not want some other class can be inherited from your class. If you created a class with a complete class definition, and you are sure that no subclass will be needed. This means you already know that the extension of your class is not needed. In these situations, you can have final class.

There are other design decisions as well that needed your class to restrict from being extended. I want to mention the example of String class, String class is immutable, you cannot extend any class from String class. Creating immutable class is more than of creating final class, but final class helps making class immutable. String class is declared as -

```
public final class String
```

As you might already know that a final variable cannot be reassigned, it should be initialized at the time of definition. A final method cannot be overridden.

Class access specifier

Only public, abstract & final are permitted for class. You can also declare class without access specifier. If you are creating public class, your class name should be same as file name, or else you will get compiler error.

```
1. public class TestPublic {
2.
3. }
```

 Above class TestPublic should be in TestPublic.java file. In the same file you can create as many classes without access specifier. There should be only one public class per .java file and that class name should be same as file name. In file

TestPublic.java you can have maximum of one public class TestPublic, and as many classes without any access specifier as below.

```
1. public class TestPublic {
2.
3. }
4.
5.   class ClassOne{
6.
7. }
8.
9. class ClassTwo{
10.
11.   }
```

Nested class

Nested class is a class inside a class. Nested class can be static nested class or inner class. Static nested class is a static class inside a class, and inner class is a non-static nested class inside a class.

Scope of nested class is depending on the scope of outer class. If you cannot access the outer class, you cannot access nested class. Nested class having access of all the members of outer class, including private class. Nested class is treated as a member of outer class. A nested class can have public, protected, private, or default access specifier.

Static nested class:

```
1. //outer class
2. class OuterClass
3. {
4.    static int a = 1;
5.
6.    int b = 2;
7.
8.    private static int c = 3;
9.
10.   // static nested class
11.   static class StaticNestedClass
12.      {
13.             void print()
14.             {
```

```
15.                    System.out.println("a = " + a);
16.
17.           //b is a non-static method and can not be accessed
   in this static nested class
18.           //System.out.println("b = " + b); //compilation
   error if uncommnted
19.
20.                    System.out.println("c = " + c);

21.                         }
22.              }
23.  }
24.
25.  public class StaticNested
26.  {
27.           public static void main(String[] args)
28.              {
29.                OuterClass.StaticNestedClass obj = new
   OuterClass.StaticNestedClass();
30.
31.              obj.print();
32.
33.              }
34.  }
```

Static nested class can access only static member of the outer class.

Inner class:

```
1. //outer class
2. class OuterClass1
3. {
4.   static int a = 1;
5.   int b = 2;
6.   private int c = 3;
7.
8.   // inner class
9.   class InnerClass
10.  {
11.    void print()
12.      {
13.          System.out.println("a = " + a);
14.
15.          System.out.println("b = " + b);
16.
17.          System.out.println("c = " + c);
18.
```

```
19.                }
20.      }
21.   }
22.
23.   public class RegularInnerClass
24.   {
25.      public static void main(String[] args)
26.      {
27.            OuterClass1 outerObject = new OuterClass1();
28.            OuterClass1.InnerClass innerObject =
      outerObject.new InnerClass();
29.
30.            innerObject.print();
31.
32.      }
33.   }
```

Inner class should be non-static that can access all the members of outer class, even private and static members. To instantiate the Inner class, first instantiate the outer class and then instantiate the inner class within the outer class instance.

A major difference between the Static Nested class and inner class is, you can have main() method in Static nested class, but you cannot have main() method in Inner class. You cannot have main() method in inner class because inner class cannot invoked directly from command line, but Static nested class can be invoked directly from command line.

Both Inner class and Static nested class is the type of Nested class, shown in figure below.

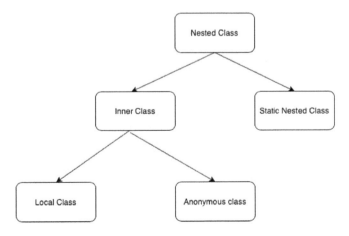

As in figure above Inner class and Static Nested class is Nested class. Inner class can be of two type Local Inner Class (Local Class) and Anonymous Class.

Local Inner Class

Local Inner class is also called just local class. This class is declared and instantiated inside method of outer class. Local Inner class can access all local variable from outer class. Before Java 8, local class was able to access only final variable of outer class, but since Java 8 onwards, local class can access final and non-final variable from outer class. Below is the example.

```
1.  //Outer Class
2.  class Outer {
3.    //Method of Outer Class
4.    void outerPrint() {
5.
6.        int a = 10;
7.        final int b = 20;
8.        //Inner Class inside method
9.      class LocalInnerClass {
10.       //Method inside local inner class
11.            void innerPrint() {
12.                //print normal variable
13.            System.out.println("a= "+a);
14.            //print final variable
15.
   System.out.println("b= "+b);
16.                            }
17.            }
18.        //Instanciate local class inside method
19.        LocalInnerClass y = new LocalInnerClass();
20.        //call of local inner class method
21.        y.innerPrint();
22.            }
23.  }
24.
25.  public class LocalClass {
26.
27.      public static void main(String[] args) {
28.
29.            Outer obj =new Outer();
30.            obj.outerPrint();
31.        }
32.  }
```

In above example, you can see the Local Inner Class was able to access final and non-final variable from outer class.

Anonymous class

Anonymous class is also called Anonymous Inner class. Anonymous class is like local inner class without name. It does not have name. Anonymous class is declared and instantiated at the same time. If you need to use local inner class only once, you can use anonymous inner class instead of local inner class.

Anonymous class is special because it can be used to extend a class, it can be used to implement an interface. Anonymous class can also be used as method arguments or inside constructor argument.

Anonymous class is short form of a class that will save lots of line of code and reduce lots of complexity. Below is the example.

```
1.  interface Animal
2.  {
3.    void sleep();
4.  }
5.
6.  class Dog implements Animal
7.  {
8.    @Override
9.    public void sleep()
10.          {
11.                  System.out.print("Dog is sleeping");
12.          }
13.  }
14.
15.
16.  class SimpleMainClass
17.  {
18.          public static void main(String[] args)
19.          {
20.              // Dog is implementation class of Animal
      interface
21.                  Dog obj=new Dog();
22.
23.              // calling sleep() method implemented at Dog
24.                  obj.sleep();
25.          }
26.  }
```

 Above is an example of code without anonymous class. Animal interface is having abstract method sleep(). Class Dog implemented the interface Animal method sleep. Now in main method it is calling implemented method sleep. Everything is fine and it will print "Dog is sleeping".

But if you use anonymous class in above code then there is no need to write one extra class Dog. You can directly declare anonymous class in main method that will implements Animal interface and provide implementation of sleep method. Below is the example.

```
1.  interface Animal
2.  {
3.    void sleep();
4.  }
5.
6.
7.  public class AnonymousClassExample
8.  {
9.    public static void main(String[] args)
10.   {
11.          // Anonymous class implementing Animal interface
12.          Animal obj=new Animal() {
13.
14.                  @Override
15.                  public void sleep() {
16.                                  System.out.println("Dog is
    sleeping");
17.                          }
18.                  };
19.
20.          // calling sleep() method implemented in anonymous
    class
21.          obj.sleep();
22.          }
23.  }
```

Above code is the same code implemented through anonymous class. As you already know here @override annotation is optional but use it as best practice.

Similarly, anonymous class can be used with class. See below example.

```
1.  abstract class Animal
2.  {
3.    public abstract void sleep();
4.  }
5.
```

```
6.
7. public class AnonymousClassExample
8. {
9.   public static void main(String[] args)
10.  {
11.          // Anonymous class implementing Animal interface
12.          Animal obj=new Animal() {
13.
14.          @Override
15.          public void sleep() {
16.                              System.out.println("Dog is
   sleeping");
17.                          }
18.          };
19.
20.          // calling sleep() method implemented in anonymous
   class
21.              obj.sleep();
22.          }
23.  }
```

Anonymous class can be passed as method arguments or constructor arguments. As constructor is also a method, I will provide an example of passing anonymous class as an argument. Similarly, you can create and pass anonymous class as an argument.

```
1. interface Animal
2. {
3.   String sleep();
4. }
5.
6.
7. public class AnonymousClassExample
8. {
9.   public static void callSleep(Animal animal) {
10.               System.out.println(animal.sleep());
11.          }
12.
13. public static void main(String[] args)
14.  {
15.          //anonymous class in argument
16.          callSleep(new Animal() {
17.
18.                  @Override
19.                  public String sleep() {
20.                          return "Dog is sleeping";
21.                          }
22.                  });
```

```
23.
24.              }
25.  }
```

Above class is having the same implementation as other example of anonymous class. It will produce the same result.

Immutable class

Immutable class is a class whose object state cannot be changed once created. Once you create an object of immutable class, you cannot change its content. All the wrapper classes like Integer, Long, Short, Boolean, Byte, etc. are immutable class. String class is also immutable class. In java.time package lots of classes like LocalDate, LocalDateTime, LocalTime, MonthDay, OffsetDateTime, OffsetTime, Year, YearMonth, and ZonedDateTime classes are immutable class.

Benefits of Immutable class

Immutable class is thread-safe by default. As you cannot change the object once created, it can be used in multithreaded environment safely. It can also be used for caching purpose as the value of immutable object cannot change.
Creating immutable class in easy.

How to create Immutable class

Keep in mind below points to create immutable class.
- Make all the fields of class as final and private so that these fields cannot be accessed from outside of class.
- Create only getter method to access fields of class. Do not provide setter method so that no one can set any value to the field.
- Restrict inheritance. Do not allow any class to extend from immutable class you are creating. You can do this in two ways. The easiest way to do this is to make the class final. The other way is to make the constructor private and construct instance in factory method.
- Initialize all the values at the time of object creation.
- Do not allow any method to modify any object.

Example of immutable class using final class.

```
1. public final class ImmutableClass
2. {
3.      private final int id;
4.      private final String name;
5.
6.       public ImmutableClass(int id, String name) {
7.           this.name = name;
8.           this.id = id;
9.       }
10.      public int getId() {
11.              return id;
12.          }
13.      public String getName() {
14.              return name;
15.          }
16.  }
```

Above is very simple example of immutable class. Now I am going to add one reference type variable in the same example and see what happens.

```
1. public final class ImmutableClass
2. {
3.      private final int id;
4.      private final String name;
5.      private final Department dept; // Department class
6.
7.       public ImmutableClass(int id, String name, Department
   dept) {
8.           this.name = name;
9.           this.id = id;
10.          this.dept = dept;   //initialization of dept
11.       }
12.      public int getId() {
13.              return id;
14.          }
15.      public String getName() {
16.              return name;
17.          }
18.      public Department getDept() {
19.                  return dept;
20.              }
21.
22.  }
```

If you will see in above class I just added (injected) department class object as final. I have created very simple Department class having just one variable departmentName as below.

```
1. public class Department {
2.    private String departmentName;
3.
4.    public String getDepartmentName() {
5.            return departmentName;
6.    }
7.
8.    public void setDepartmentName(String departmentName) {
9.            this.departmentName = departmentName;
10.           }
11. }
```

What do you think? `ImmutableClass` is still immutable? No, it is no more immutable. Let's try to change the object and see if it is changed.

```
1. public class ImmutableMain {
2.
3.    public static void main(String[] args) {
4.       //department Object
5.       Department dept = new Department();
6.       dept.setDepartmentName("One");
7.
8.       //immutable object
9.       ImmutableClass obj = new ImmutableClass(1, "Ashu",
   dept);
10.
11.      System.out.println("Department before modification = " +
   obj.getDept().getDepartmentName());
12.
13.      //try to change department name
14.      dept.setDepartmentName("Two");
15.
16.      System.out.println("Department after modification = " +
   obj.getDept().getDepartmentName());
17.           }
18.
19.  }
```

Output:

```
Department before modification = One
Department after modification = Two
```

Modified. This is no more immutable, and I am able to change the object. Let's fix this to make this class as immutable.

```
1.  public final class ImmutableClass
2.  {
3.      private final int id;
4.      private final String name;
5.      private final Department dept; // Department class
6.
7.    public ImmutableClass(int id, String name, Department
    dept) {
8.          this.name = name;
9.          this.id = id;
10.         this.dept = new Department();
11.
    this.dept.setDepartmentName(dept.getDepartmentName());
12.  }
13.   public int getId() {
14.             return id;
15.          }
16.   public String getName() {
17.             return name;
18.          }
19.    public Department getDept() {
20.                return dept;
21.            }
22.
23.  }
```

 I have modified `ImmutableClass`, now department object initialization will not update the same object. By keeping the department class and main method same, with this modified Immutable Class the output of same program will be –

```
Department before modification = One
Department after modification = One
```

You can see the output above; you are no more able to change the object. Now this class is immutable.

String Class

String class is immutable class in Java. String works differently. For String there is separate kind of memory in heap called String constant pool. String will store in String constant pool only if you will create string using string literal.

String can be created using two ways – using String literal and using new keyword. Creating string using String literal is as –

```
String str1 = "Hello";
String str2 = "Hello";
```

Above two string str1 and str2 are created using string literal. Here both str1 and str2 gets created in String constant pool in heap. Because value of str1 and str2 is same it both will point to the same memory.

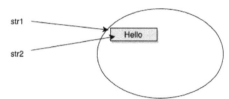

As you see in above representation that str1 and str2 is pointing to the same memory, as it is like a same object with two different names. Now let's change the value of str2: `str2 = "Hi";` Now str2 is different object. Every time you change the value of string it creates a new object with new memory location. After changing the value of str2, str1 will keep pointing the same memory but str2 will start pointing a different location in heap memory.

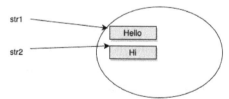

Creating String with `new` operator is similar to the creating a normal class object that will be stored in normal heap. If you create String like –

```
String str3 = new String("Hello");
```

The object str3 will get created in normal heap memory not in the constant pool. In that way str1 and str3 both is having same value but will point to two different memory location. String str1 will be stored in String constant pool inside heap memory and str3 will get stored in normal (non-pool) heap memory.

Object class

Object class is base class of all the class in java. Every class extends Object class, even though we do not write extends Object in class definition. Any class that you create implicitly extends the Object class. In that way Object class functionality is present in every class in java.

Below are the methods provided by Object class that you can override in your class for overriding with your own implementation.

Clone method

Clone method creates and return a copy of this object. To use this method your class must implements Cloneable interface.

```java
1. public class Student{
2.
3.     private Integer id;
4.     private String name;
5.
6.     public Integer getId() {
7.             return id;
8.     }
9.     public void setId(Integer id) {
10.                 this.id = id;
11.             }
12.     public String getName() {
13.                     return name;
14.             }
15.     public void setName(String name) {
16.                     this.name = name;
17.             }
18.
19.     public static void main(String[] args) throws
    CloneNotSupportedException {
20.
21.             Student obj = new Student();
22.             obj.setId(1);
23.             obj.setName("Ashu");
24.
25.             Student cloneObj = (Student) obj.clone();
26.
27.             System.out.println(cloneObj.getId());
28.
29.                     System.out.println(cloneObj.getName());
```

```
30.
31.            }
32.
33.  }
```

 Above code will throw below exception as Cloneable interface is not implemented.

```
Exception in thread "main" java.lang.CloneNotSupportedException:
```

Let's see how it works if you implement Cloneable interface.

```
1. public class Student implements Cloneable{
2.
3.    private Integer id;
4.    private String name;
5.
6.    public Integer getId() {
7.           return id;
8.    }
9.    public void setId(Integer id) {
10.               this.id = id;
11.          }
12.   public String getName() {
13.               return name;
14.          }
15.   public void setName(String name) {
16.               this.name = name;
17.          }
18.
19.   public static void main(String[] args) throws
   CloneNotSupportedException {
20.
21.          Student obj = new Student();
22.          obj.setId(1);
23.          obj.setName("Ashu");
24.
25.          Student cloneObj = (Student) obj.clone();
26.
27.          System.out.println(cloneObj.getId());
28.
29.                System.out.println(cloneObj.getName());
30.
31.          }
32.
33.  }
```

Output:
```
1
Ashu
```
In above example Student object is successfully coned and printed the same value.

hashCode method

The hashCode method returns an integer hashcode for an object generated by a hashing algorithm. Objects that are equal must return the same hashcode. Most of the IDE provides the feature of generating hashcode and equals based on the selected fields of class. Below is the example of hashcode generated based on integer field id.

```
1.  @Override
2.  public int hashCode() {
3.      final int prime = 31;
4.      int result = 1;
5.      result = prime * result + ((id == null) ? 0 :
    id.hashCode());
6.      return result;
7.  }
```

Or you can return a constant based on your need like –

```
1.  @Override
2.  public int hashCode() {
3.          return 1;
4.  }
```

It depends how you want your object will get compared.

equals method

The equals method indicates if some other object is equal to this object. If objects are equal, then it returns true or else it returns false. Like hashCode most of the IDE like eclipse and IntelliJ provides the way to generate equals method with hashCode method.

Below is the example of equals method overridden that consider id variable to check if two objects are equal.

```
1.    @Override
2.    public boolean equals(Object obj) {
```

```
3.        if (this == obj)
4.                return true;
5.        if (obj == null)
6.                return false;
7.        if (getClass() != obj.getClass())
8.                return false;
9.        Student other = (Student) obj;
10.       if (id == null) {
11.          if (other.id != null)
12.            return false;
13.          } else if (!id.equals(other.id))
14.                return true;
15.          }
```

Above code checks if both objects are same object or value of id variable in both the object is same, then both provided object and this object is equal.

finalize method

The finalize method of Object class gets called by garbage collector when garbage collector determines that there is no more reference to the object. You can override finalize method in your class if you want to perform some cleanup before object get garbage collected. You can override this method in your class and write all the cleanup code for disposing the resources if needed.

```
1. @Override
2. protected void finalize() throws Throwable {
3.   // reader.close()
4.   //do all the cleanup
5. }
```

toString method

The toString method returns the String representation of object. You can override toString method in your class for your own implementation like below.

```
1. @Override
2. public String toString() {
3.    return "Student [id=" + id + ", name=" + name + "]";
4. }
```

wait method

The wait method cause current thread to wait until other method invokes notify() or notifyAll(). There is overloaded wait() method available. The wait() method without an argument just wait until some other thread will call notify() or notifyAll() . The wait(long timeout) will cause the current thread to wait until notify() or notifyAll() will be called by other thread or timeout occurs.

notify method

The notify() method wakes up a single thread that is waiting on this objects monitor. If multiple thread on this object are waiting, then one of the threads will be chosen to awaken. The notifyAll() wakes up all the thread waiting on the objects monitor.

Object Comparisons

There are ways to compare objects. It depends what you want to compare while comparing two objects. You may want to know if both are the same object, means reference of both objects is same. You may want to know if all the values of the both objects are same. You may override the hashCode() and equals() methods to check, if certain field values of both objects are same then objects are same. Below is the way to compare.

The == and != operator

You can use this operator to see if object is null or an object is not null.

```
1.           if(obj == null) {
2.                   // create object
3.               }
```

Or you can check for not null.

```
1.           if(obj != null) {
2.                   // dp something
3.               }
```

You can do object comparison to check if both object references are to the same object.

```
1.  if(obj == obj2) {
2.    System.out.println("Both objects are same");
3.  }else {
4.    System.out.println("Both objects are different");
5.  }
```

You can check if two Enum values are same with equal operator (==), as there is only one object for each Enum object.

equals() method

The equals() method is used to compare object for equality. This method is provided by Object class. You have to override this method in your class for your specific implementation, Object class version do not provide you precise result.

```
1.  if(obj.equals(obj2)) {
2.    System.out.println("Both object is same");
3.  }else {
4.    System.out.println("Both objects are different");
5.  }
```

If both object equality checked and found equals as per implementation, then it returns true. Let's say you have Person class having name, dateOfBirth, and address fields in the Person class. Your explanation of equality of Person object is, if Person's name and dateOfBirth is same then both Person is same. In this case you can override the equals method and compare for name and dateOfBirth and if both are same return true. Now if two Person object is having same value for name and dateOfBirth then it will return true saying both objects are equal. Below is the implementation.

```
1.  public class Person {
2.
3.    private String name;
4.    private String dateOfBith;
5.    private String address;
6.
7.    public String getName() {
8.            return name;
9.    }
10.   public void setName(String name) {
11.              this.name = name;
```

```
12.              }
13.    public String getDateOfBith() {
14.                  return dateOfBith;
15.              }
16.    public void setDateOfBith(String dateOfBith) {
17.                  this.dateOfBith = dateOfBith;
18.              }
19.    public String getAddress() {
20.                  return address;
21.              }
22.    public void setAddress(String address) {
23.                  this.address = address;
24.              }
25.
26.    @Override
27.    public boolean equals(Object obj) {
28.          if (this == obj)
29.                  return true;
30.          if (obj == null)
31.                  return false;
32.          if (getClass() != obj.getClass())
33.                  return false;
34.          Person other = (Person) obj;
35.          if (dateOfBith == null) {
36.                  if (other.dateOfBith != null)
37.                          return false;
38.          } else if (!dateOfBith.equals(other.dateOfBith))
39.                  return false;
40.          if (name == null) {
41.                  if (other.name != null)
42.                          return false;
43.          } else if (!name.equals(other.name))
44.                  return false;
45.                  return true;
46.          }
47.  }
```

Person class implemented the overridden method equals() that checks if name and dateOfBith is same then person object is same. Now test this class.

```
1. public static void main(String[] args) {
2.
3.    Person person1 = new Person();
4.    person1.setName("Ashu");
5.    person1.setDateOfBith("Jul-05-2020");
6.    person1.setAddress("Atlanta");
7.
```

```
8.    Person person2 = new Person();
9.    person2.setName("Ashu");
10.   person2.setDateOfBith("Jul-05-2020");
11.   person2.setAddress("New York");
12.
13.   if(person1.equals(person2)) {
14.         System.out.println("Same Person");
15.   }else {
16.         System.out.println("Different Person");
17.     }
18.   }
```

Output:
```
Same Person
```

You can see objects are equal here because name and dateOfBirth is same even though address is different. But if name or dateOfBirth is different then object will be considered different. See below.

```
1. public static void main(String[] args) {
2.
3.    Person person1 = new Person();
4.    person1.setName("Ashu");
5.    person1.setDateOfBith("Jul-05-2020");
6.    person1.setAddress("Atlanta");
7.
8.    Person person2 = new Person();
9.    person2.setName("Neha");
10.   person2.setDateOfBith("Jul-05-2020");
11.   person2.setAddress("New York");
12.
13.   if(person1.equals(person2)) {
14.         System.out.println("Same Person");
15.   }else {
16.         System.out.println("Different Person");
17.           }
18.   }
```

Output:
```
Different Person
```

In above code I changed the name, and now both objects are not same.

Comparable interface

Comparable interface provide compareTo() method that returns integer value to tells if the value compared is less than, equal to or greater than. See below example.

```
1. public class Person implements Comparable<Person>{
2.
3.    String name;
4.    Integer personId;
5.
6.    public Person(String name, Integer personId) {
7.            super();
8.            this.name = name;
9.            this.personId = personId;
10.           }
11.
12.  public int compareTo(Person obj){
13.          if(personId==obj.personId)
14.          return 0;
15.          else if(personId>obj.personId)
16.          return 1;
17.          else
18.          return -1;
19.          }
20.  }
```

In above example code, class Person implements Comparable interface and overrides compareTo() method on comparison of personId.

```
1. public static void main(String[] args) {
2.
3.    ArrayList<Person> personList = new ArrayList<>();
4.    personList.add(new Person("Ashu",25));
5.    personList.add(new Person("Neha",15));
6.    personList.add(new Person("Prince",18));
7.
8.    Collections.sort(personList);
9.
10.  for(Person p:personList){
11.     System.out.println(p.name+" "+p.personId);
12.  }
13.
14.  }
```

Output:
```
Neha 15
Prince 18
Ashu 25
```

Above code will sort the object based on personId. Collection.sort() method use compareTo() method of object to compare the object and sorted objects based on personId.

Comparator interface

Comparator interface having abstract method compare(Object, Object) that is used to compare two objects. You need to create separate comparator class that implements Comparator interface to compare two objects. In this case, in sort() method you will provide the name of comparator class so that sort() method knows how to compare objects. See below the same example with comparator.

```
1. public class Person{
2.
3.    String name;
4.    Integer personId;
5.
6.    public Person(String name, Integer personId) {
7.            super();
8.            this.name = name;
9.            this.personId = personId;
10.           }
11.   }
```

Above is the Person class having personId and name. Now create a comparator class as below.

```
1. public class PersonComparator implements Comparator<Person>
      {
2.
3.    @Override
4.    public int compare(Person p1, Person p2) {
5.            if(p1.personId==p2.personId)
6.            return 0;
7.            else if(p1.personId>p2.personId)
8.            return 1;
```

```
9.          else
10.                 return -1;
11.         }
12.  }
```

PersonComparator class comparing object in the same way we have implemented for comparable interface. It is comparing personId to compare object. Now below is the use.

```
1. public static void main(String[] args) {
2.
3.    ArrayList<Person> personList = new ArrayList<>();
4.    personList.add(new Person("Ashu",25));
5.    personList.add(new Person("Neha",15));
6.    personList.add(new Person("Prince",18));
7.
8.    Collections.sort(personList,new PersonComparator());
9.
10.           for(Person p:personList){
11.           System.out.println(p.name+" "+p.personId);
12.           }
13.
14.  }
```

Output:
```
Neha 15
Prince 18
Ashu 25
```

You can see above that I am providing the comparator class in Collections.sort() method as second argument.

enumerations

The Enum type is a special data type or a special class that represents group of constants. The Enum can have constructor and methods. See the example below.

```
1. public class ColorMain {
2.
3.    public static void main(String[] args) {
4.
5.            Color obj = Color.RED;
6.
```

```
7.              System.out.println(obj);
8.
9.              obj.colorInfo();
10.           }
11.  }
12.
13.  enum Color {
14.          BLUE,
15.          RED,
16.          YELLOW,
17.          GREEN;
18.
19.    Color() {
20.         System.out.println("Constructor called for color: "+
     this.toString());
21.              }
22.
23.    public void colorInfo()
24.      {
25.        System.out.println("Color is: "+ this.toString());
26.      }
27.
28.  }
```

Output:
```
Constructor called for color: BLUE
Constructor called for color: RED
Constructor called for color: YELLOW
Constructor called for color: GREEN
RED
Color is: RED
```

In above example Enum Color defined the color constants. You can see constructor gets called for each constant. I am using to print one of the constant whose value is RED. Also calling the method using RED color constant. You can define other method similarly.

Generics

Generic in java is similar to the template in C++. Generics introduced in java since JDK 5.0. A class, interface, or method that operate on a data type that is provided as a parameter is called generics. Generics means parameterized types.

The best example of generics are the collection classes. For example, you use List with the type parameter like List<String>, List<Integer>, List<Person>, etc. With generics it is possible for List class to operate on different data types or else a separate List class would be needed for each data type. Below are the examples.

Advantage of generics is reusability. You can reuse same code for different data type. Other advantage is type safety, as generics are substituted at **compile time** it ensures type safety.

Generic class

Generic class is a class that can accept parameters of different type. See example below.

```
1.  //Generic class with generic type T
2.  class GenericClass<T>
3.  {
4.    //variable of type T
5.    T obj;
6.
7.    // initialize variable in constructor
8.    GenericClass(T obj) { this.obj = obj; }
9.
10.
11.   //method returns value of T
12.   public T getValue() { return this.obj; }
13.   }
14.
15.   public class GenericsTest
16.   {
17.     public static void main (String[] args)
18.     {
19.       // Use Integer type
20.       GenericClass <Integer> intObj = new
    GenericClass<Integer>(10);
21.
22.       System.out.println(intObj.getValue());
23.
24.        // use String type
25.       GenericClass <String> strObj =
26.           new GenericClass<String>("Hello Generics");
27.
28.        System.out.println(strObj.getValue());
29.
30.         // use Person type
31.         GenericClass <Person> personObj =
32.         new GenericClass<Person>(new Person("Ashu", 101));
33.
34.   System.out.println("name: "+personObj.getValue().name +",
    personId: "+personObj.getValue().personId);
```

```
35.              }
36.  }
```

Output:
```
10
Hello Generics
name: Ashu, personId: 101
```

Above Generic class can accept any type. In above example I have passed integer, string, and Person type. Person type (Person class) is as below.

```
1. public class Person{
2.
3.     String name;
4.     Integer personId;
5.
6.     public Person(String name, Integer personId) {
7.             super();
8.             this.name = name;
9.             this.personId = personId;
10.            }
11.  }
```

In generics, you can define multiple generic parameters. See example below that the same class can have more than one parameter. Example is with two generic parameters below.

```
1.  //Generic class with generic type T
2.  class GenericClass<T, U>
3.  {
4.    //variable of type T & U
5.    T objT;
6.    U objU;
7.
8.    // initialize variable in constructor
9.    GenericClass(T objT, U objU)
10.          {
11.                  this.objT = objT;
12.                  this.objU = objU;
13.          }
14.
15.
16.   //method returns value of T
17.   public T getTValue() { return this.objT; }
18.
```

```
19.  //method returns value of U
20.  public U getUValue() { return this.objU; }
21.  }
22.
23.  public class GenericsTest
24.  {
25.    public static void main (String[] args)
26.    {
27.       // Use Integer, Integer type
28.       GenericClass <Integer, Integer> intObj = new
   GenericClass<>(10, 20);
29.
30.  System.out.println("T value: "+intObj.getTValue()+ ", U
   value: "+intObj.getUValue());
31.
32.  // use Integer, String type
33.  GenericClass <Integer, String> strObj =
34.         new GenericClass<>(30, "Hello Generics");
35.
36.  System.out.println("T value: "+strObj.getTValue()+", U
   value: "+strObj.getUValue());
37.
38.  // use Integer, Person type
39.  GenericClass <Integer, Person> personObj =
40.  new GenericClass<>(40, new Person("Ashu", 101));
41.
42.  System.out.println("T value: "+personObj.getTValue() +", U
   value: "+personObj.getUValue().name+ "
   "+personObj.getUValue().personId);
43.              }
44.  }
```

Output:
```
T value: 10, U value: 20
T value: 30, U value: Hello Generics
T value: 40, U value: Ashu 101
```

Similarly, you can have n number of generic parameters for class. In same way you can use generics for interface.

Generic methods

You can use generics for methods by passing generic type arguments in method and generic return type as well. In the above class example, you can see method getValue, getTValue, and getUValue have generic return type. Also, you can see in above generic class example that constructor is having generic type arguments, as constructor is a method, you can use generic arguments in the same way.

```
1. public class GenericMethod {
2.
3.    static <T> void genericMethod (T obj) {
4.
5.        System.out.println("Object type is:
   "+obj.getClass().getName());
6.        System.out.println("Object value is: "+obj);
7.    }
8.
9.   public static void main(String[] args) {
10.
11.           //call method with integer
12.           genericMethod(10);
13.
14.           //call method with string
15.           genericMethod("Hello generic method");
16.
17.           //call generic method with Person
18.           genericMethod(new Person("Ashu", 101));
19.
20.
21.           }
22.
23.   }
```

Output:
```
Object type is: java.lang.Integer
Object value is: 10
Object type is: java.lang.String
Object value is: Hello generic method
Object type is: ashu.tech.classobjects.Person
Object value is: ashu.tech.classobjects.Person@d716361
```

In above code, generic method arguments can be of any type.

Exception handling

An exception can be defined as an event that occurs during execution of program and disrupts the normal flow of execution.

When an error occurs within a method, the method creates an exception object and hands it off to the runtime system. After a method throws an exception the runtime system attempts to find something (exception handler) to handle it. Runtime system searches the call stack for a exception handler method.

Try-catch and throw

Putting code in try catch block is the way to provide exception handler in catch block for the code enclosed in try block. If you decided to throw an exception, it goes to the parent method, and it is parent method's responsibility to either put this method call in try-catch block or re-throw the exception again its parent method.

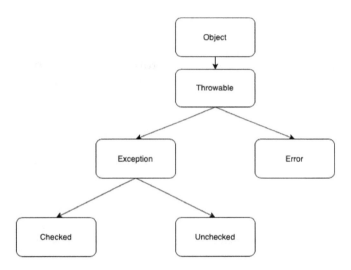

Exception can be of two type, checked and unchecked exception. Error and exception share the same parent class.

Error

Error is irrecoverable that you cannot handle. Error could be any virtual machine error, Stack overflow error, or OutOfMemoryError.

Checked Exception

Checked exception is all the exception except RunTimeException. Checked exceptions are checked at compile time. Checked exceptions are the exception that are required to check with the try and catch block. You may have seen that using any method required you to handle that exception either in try-catch or re-throw that exception. Those are checked exceptions. Checked exception is expected to occur. For example, IOException or FileNotFoundException.

Unchecked exception

Unchecked exceptions are the run-time exception that is because of some bug in a code. It is normally suggested that let the system break itself without handling of run-time exceptions. Unchecked exception examples are NullPointerException, AirthmeticException etc.

User Defined Exception Class

You can define your own exception class to catch or re-throw custom exception. To define your own Exception class extend your exception class from Exception class as below.

```
1.  class MyException extends Exception
2.  {
3.    MyException() { }
4.
5.    // one argument constructor
6.    MyException(String str) { super(str); }
7.
8.    public static void main(String[] args)
9.    {
10.      try {
11.           int i =11;
12.           if(i>10) {
13.           MyException me = new MyException("Greater than 10
    exception");
14.           throw me;
15.        }
16.   } catch (MyException e) {
17.                e.printStackTrace();
18.        }
19.      }
20.  }
```

Exception:
```
MyException: Greater than 10 exception
```

In above example MyException is user defined exception class.

Annotations

Annotations are the decorators in java construct that can be used with class, method, or fields. Annotation cannot execute any code by themselves. It can be used by compiler or runtime framework to perform certain action. For example, @Autowired annotation change the runtime behavior of a program. Annotation can have parameters as well.

User-defined Annotation

To define your own annotation, you can create new annotation similar to creating new class in IDE.

Below is the example of creating field annotation

```
1. @Retention(RetentionPolicy.RUNTIME)
2. @Target(ElementType.FIELD)
3. public @interface StringInitializer {
4.
5.   public String value() default "";
6. }
```

While creating annotation the method should have no parameter and should not throw any exception. The return type is restricted to primitive, like String, Class, Enums, annotations, and Arrays. The default value of annotation cannot be null.

5 Java Collection

Java collection framework is a combination of classes and interface which is used to store and manage group of objects. In this chapter we will talk about collections, map, iterator and other interfaces and classes. Let's discuss about each term in details.

Collection Framework Hierarchy

Below is the hierarchy of collection framework.

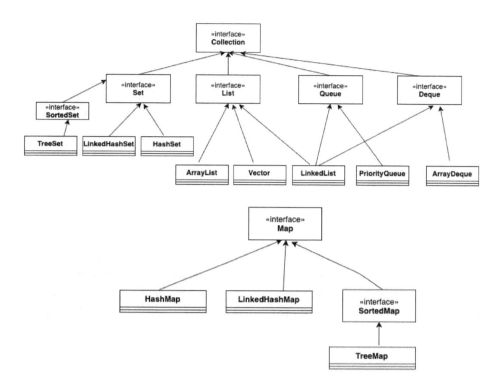

Enumeration

Enumeration is an interface that is used to iterate the legacy collections like vector and HashTable. Enumeration was the first iterator introduced in java. It have basically two methods, hasMoreElements() and nextElement(). Below is the example of Enumeration used to iterate vector.

```
1. public class EnumerationTest
2. {
3.   public static void main(String[] args)
4.   {
5.     // create and add element in vector
6.     Vector<Integer> v = new Vector<>();
7.     for (int i = 0; i < 10; i++) {
8.         v.addElement(i);
9.     }
10.    //Print vector
11.    System.out.println(v);
12.
```

```
13.    // e will point to the index just before the first
   element in v
14.    Enumeration<Integer> e = v.elements();
15.
16.    // while next element available
17.    while (e.hasMoreElements())
18.    {
19.      // move cursor to the next element
20.      int i = (Integer)e.nextElement();
21.
22.      //print each element with a space
23.      System.out.print(i + " ");
24.              }
25.    }
26.  }
```

In above example Enumeration is being used to iterate the vector to print its value. Enumeration works on vector and HashTable, it is not a universal iterator. You cannot perform remove operation using Enumeration. You can iterate in forward direction only using Enumeration.

Iterator

Iterator is used to iterate through the elements in collections framework. Iterator is improved from Enumeration and it can be used to read or remove operation. Iterator is available for all the collection interfaces and classes as well as map interface. You can get iterator by calling iterator() method on any collection object. It has hasNext(), next(), and remove() method. Iterator also works only in forward direction. You cannot replace or add new element through iterator.

Below is the example of iterator on List.

```
1. public class IteratorTest
2. {
3.   public static void main(String[] args)
4.   {
5.     List<Integer> numList = new ArrayList<>();
6.
7.     // Add element to List
8.     for (int i = 0; i < 10; i++)
9.           numList.add(i);
10.
11.     // it points to index just before the first element of
   numList
```

```
12.     Iterator<Integer> it = numList.iterator();
13.
14.     // while next element is available
15.     while (it.hasNext())
16.             {
17.     // move to next element of numList
18.     int i = (Integer)it.next();
19.
20.     // print each element
21.     System.out.print(i + " ");
22.
23.     // Remove odd element
24.     if (i % 2 != 0)
25.             it.remove();
26.  }
27.     System.out.println();
28.     //print final numList after removal of odd
29.      System.out.println(numList);
30.      }
31.  }
```

Output:
```
0 1 2 3 4 5 6 7 8 9
[0, 2, 4, 6, 8]
```

 Above is the example of iterator iterating through a list and removing the odd numbers from the list.

ListIterator

ListIterator is a special type of iterator that can be used for only classes implementing the List interface like ArrayList or LinkedList. ListIterator has more functionality than the iterator, like ListIterator can move in both forward and backward direction. Also, ListIterator can replace the element and add the element in List, the normal iterator is not having that capability.

ListIterator provides below methods to help in iterator and do operation on List. Below is the example of ListIterator.

```
1. public class ListIteratorTest
2. {
3.   public static void main(String[] args)
```

```
4.    {
5.       ArrayList<Integer> numList = new ArrayList<>();
6.       for (int i = 0; i < 10; i++)
7.             numList.add(i);
8.
9.       ListIterator<Integer> ltr = numList.listIterator();
10.
11.      // forward iteration
12.      while (ltr.hasNext())
13.      {
14.        // next element
15.        int i = (Integer)ltr.next();
16.
17.        // print next element
18.        System.out.print(i + " ");
19.
20.        // Changing even numbers to odd by replacing using set
21.        if (i%2==0)
22.        {
23.            i++;
24.            ltr.set(i);
25.        }
26.      }
27.      System.out.println();
28.      //print list after replacing all even with odd
29.      System.out.println(numList);
30.
31.      //backward iteration
32.      while (ltr.hasPrevious())
33.      {
34.        // previous element
35.        int i = (Integer)ltr.previous();
36.
37.        // print previous element- will be printed in backward
   direction
38.        System.out.print(i + " ");
39.
40.      }
41.    }
42.  }
```

Output:
```
0 1 2 3 4 5 6 7 8 9
[1, 1, 3, 3, 5, 5, 7, 7, 9, 9]
9 9 7 7 5 5 3 3 1 1
```

In above example you can see working of list iterator.

Now let's go through each interface from collection hierarchy.

List Interface

List is an ordered collection that keep the elements in sequence. You will have control over where the elements in list will be inserted. You can access elements using index or position. List can have duplicate elements. List interface supports ListIterator that I have already explained. Let's have some example of List interface.

ArrayList

ArrayList is a dynamic array which size will get incremented with the growing array. ArrayList implements List interface and having implementation of all the functionality the List interface provides. If you compare ArrayList with array, then ArrayList may be slower but loaded with more functionality.

```
1.  class ArrayListTest {
2.    public static void main(String[] args)
3.    {
4.      int n = 10;
5.
6.      // List with initial size n
7.      List<Integer> fixedList
8.                  = new ArrayList<Integer>(n);
9.
10.     for (int i = 1; i <= n; i++)
11.         fixedList.add(i);
12.
13.     // Print elements
14.     System.out.println(fixedList);
15.
16.     // Remove element from index 2
17.     fixedList.remove(2);
18.
19.     // print list after deletion
20.     System.out.println(fixedList);
21.
22.     // Print each element
23.     for (int i = 0; i < fixedList.size(); i++)
24.                     System.out.print(fixedList.get(i) +
    " ");
25.
```

```
26.     //ArrayList with dynamic size
27.     List<Integer> list = new ArrayList<>();
28.     for(int i=0; i<5; i++) {
29.          list.add(i);
30.     }
31.     System.out.println();
32.          System.out.println(list);
33.     }
34.  }
```

Above example demonstrate the ArrayList.

LinkedList

LinkedList implements List interface. LinkedList is a data structure where elements stored in continuous memory locations. Every element is a separate object with a data part and address part. Elements are linked with the next element with the pointer to the address. Because of continuous memory location, searching in LinkedList is a linear search that is not the index-based search. ArrayList find operation will be faster if you know the index, in LinkedList insertion will be faster than ArrayList as you do not need to rearrange the whole List. In LinkedList each element is known as node. For frequent insertion and deletion, you can prefer LinkedList over array.

```
1. class LinkedListTest {
2.
3.   public static void main(String[] args)
4.   {
5.      int n = 5;
6.
7.      List<Integer> linkedList = new LinkedList<Integer>();
8.
9.      // Append new element at the end of the list
10.     for (int i = 1; i <= n; i++)
11.          linkedList.add(i);
12.
13.     // Print all elements
14.     System.out.println(linkedList);
15.
16.     // Remove element from index 3
17.     linkedList.remove(3);
18.
19.     // print all elements after deletion
20.     System.out.println(linkedList);
21.
```

```
22.     // iterate and print each element
23.     for (int i = 0; i < linkedList.size(); i++)
24.                     System.out.print(linkedList.get(i)
  + " ");
25.     }
26.  }
```

Set Interface

Set is a collection that does not store any duplicate elements. Set store only unique elements. If you try to add a new element to the set, set checks if the element you wanted to add is already exist. If the element already exists, then it will not add that duplicate element to the set. Set provides add method that accepts element as an argument and returns boolean. If add is successful add method returns true and if add fails because of duplicate element it will not add and return false.

HashSet

HashSet is an implementation of hash table data structure. If you insert elements in HashSet, there is no guarantee that elements will be in the same order as inserted or in any other order. HashSet allow you to insert null, as Set does not allow duplicates, you can insert at most one null. Below is the example of HashSet.

```
1. public class HashSetTest {
2.
3.   public static void main(String[] args) {
4.
5.     Set<String> colorSet = new HashSet<>();
6.
7.     Boolean result = colorSet.add("Blue");
8.     System.out.println(result);
9.
10.    result = colorSet.add("Green");
11.    System.out.println(result);
12.
13.    result = colorSet.add("Yellow");
14.    System.out.println(result);
15.
16.    result = colorSet.add("Green"); //duplicate ignored by
   Set
17.    System.out.println(result); // false
18.
19.    colorSet.remove("Yellow"); // removed Yellow
```

```
20.
21.     //print color from set
22.     for(String color: colorSet) {
23.             System.out.print(color + " ");
24.     }
25.
26.   }
27.
28. }
```

Output:
```
true
true
true
false
Blue Green
```

In above example Set is not allowing to insert Green twice. And removed Yellow after inserted. Set provides methods like addAll() to add all the elements in list at once, retainAll() that keeps all common elements of two sets, and removeAll() to remove specified elements at once. See example below.

```
1. public class HashSetTest {
2.
3.   public static void main(String[] args) {
4.
5.     Set<String> colorSetOne = new HashSet<>();
6.
     colorSetOne.addAll(Arrays.asList("Blue","Red","Green"));
     // add all adds all at once
7.
8.     Set<String> colorSetTwo = new HashSet<>();
9.
     colorSetTwo.addAll(Arrays.asList("Blue","Yellow","Orange")
     );
10.
11.     Set<String> unionSet = new HashSet<>(colorSetOne); //
     Set created with exiting colorSetOne values
12.     unionSet.addAll(colorSetTwo); // Union of colorSetOne
     and colorSetTwo, all distinct elements
13.
14.     //print union set elements
15.     for(String color: unionSet) {
16.             System.out.print(color + " ");
17.     }
18.     System.out.println(""); // new line
```

```
19.
20.     Set<String> commonSet = new HashSet<>(colorSetOne); //
   Set created with exiting colorSetOne values
21.     commonSet.retainAll(colorSetTwo); // common
   (intersection) of colorSetOne and colorSetTwo
22.
23.     //print commonSet elements
24.     for(String color: commonSet) {
25.       System.out.print(color + " ");
26.     }
27.     System.out.println(""); // new line
28.
29.     Set<String> diffSet = new HashSet<>(colorSetOne); // Set
   created with exiting colorSetOne values
30.     diffSet.removeAll(colorSetTwo); // difference of
   colorSetOne and colorSetTwo
31.
32.     //print diffSet elements
33.     for(String color: diffSet) {
34.                 System.out.print(color + " ");
35.     }
36.     System.out.println(""); // new line
37.
38.   }
39. }
```

Output:
```
Red Blue Yellow Orange Green
Blue
Red Green
```

In above example you can see how you can use set to take union, intersection (common) and difference of elements in two sets.

LinkedHashSet

LinkedHashSet is the implementation of doubly linked list that maintains the order of insertion across all elements. HashSet does not guarantee the order of elements. If you have requirement where you have to iterate the element in same order you have inserted and should not allow the duplicate elements, then LinkedHashSet is the option. LinkedHashSet maintained the order and do not allow duplicate element to be inserted.

```
1.  public class LinkedHashSetTest {
2.
3.    public static void main(String[] args) {
4.
5.       Set<String> colorSet = new LinkedHashSet<>();
6.
7.       colorSet.add("Blue");
8.       colorSet.add("Green");
9.       colorSet.add("Yellow");
10.      colorSet.add("Red");
11.
12.      colorSet.add("Green"); //duplicate ignored by Set
13.
14.      System.out.println(colorSet); /// print the set to check
     order
15.
16.      colorSet.remove("Yellow"); // removed Yellow
17.
18.      System.out.println(colorSet); /// print the set after
     removal to check order
19.
20.      }
21.
22.  }
```

Output:
```
[Blue, Green, Yellow, Red]
[Blue, Green, Red]
```

TreeSet

TreeSet implements SortedSet interface and SortedSet interface extends Set interface.
TreeSet use Tree data structure to store element, it stores elements in ascending sorted
order. When you iterate the data, it will iterate into the ascending order. You can also
iterate in descending order by using descendingIterator. See the example below.

```
1.  public class TreeSetTest {
2.
3.    public static void main(String[] args) {
4.
5.       Set<String> colorSet = new TreeSet<>();
6.
7.       colorSet.add("White");
8.       colorSet.add("Yellow");
9.       colorSet.add("Red");
```

```
10.     colorSet.add("Green");
11.     colorSet.add("Blue");
12.
13.     colorSet.add("Green"); //duplicate ignored by Set
14.
15.     System.out.println(colorSet); /// print the set to check
   order
16.
17.     colorSet.remove("Yellow"); // removed Yellow
18.
19.     System.out.println(colorSet); /// print the set after
   removal to check order
20.
21.     }
22.
23.  }
```

Output:
```
[Blue, Green, Red, White, Yellow]
[Blue, Green, Red, White]
```

In above example you can see TreeSet sorts the strings inserted. Now Let's say you are inserting Student object in TreeSet, Student object contains student id, student name, and student address. See below example.

```
1. public class TreeSetSortTest {
2.
3.   public static void main(String[] args) {
4.
5.     Student student1 = new Student(101, "Bob", "Atlanta");
6.     Student student2 = new Student(102, "Alex", "Lake Mary");
7.     Student student3 = new Student(103, "John", "Phoenix");
8.
9.     Set<Student> studentSet = new TreeSet<>();
10.     studentSet.add(student1);
11.     studentSet.add(student2);
12.     studentSet.add(student3);
13.
14.     for(Student s: studentSet) {
15.                     System.out.println(s.toString());
16.     }
17.
18.   }
19.
20.  }
21.
```

```
22.  class Student{
23.
24.     private Integer id;
25.     private String name;
26.     private String address;
27.
28.     public Student(Integer id, String name, String address)
   {
29.          super();
30.          this.id = id;
31.          this.name = name;
32.          this.address = address;
33.     }
34.
35.     @Override
36.     public String toString() {
37.          return "Student [id=" + id + ", name=" + name + ",
   address=" + address + "]";
38.     }
39.  }
```

Output:
```
Exception in thread "main" java.lang.ClassCastException: class
ashu.tech.collections.Student cannot be cast to class
java.lang.Comparable (ashu.tech.collections.Student is in unnamed
module of loader 'app'; java.lang.Comparable is in module
java.base of loader 'bootstrap')
at java.base/java.util.TreeMap.compare(TreeMap.java:1291)
at java.base/java.util.TreeMap.put(TreeMap.java:536)
at java.base/java.util.TreeSet.add(TreeSet.java:255)
at
ashu.tech.collections.TreeSetSortTest.main(TreeSetSortTest.java:1
5)
```

Above code throws an exception. It is trying to compare the object when it call the add() method to add element. As you know TreeSet is the implementation of tree data structure, and when it inserts the elements it compares the elements and insert in the sorted order. For Student object TreeSet doesn't know how to compare Student object.

There is a way to resolve this issue. Implements Comparable interface from Student class and implement compare method. Now TreeSet will get to know how to compare the Student objects. Below is the example where I am comparing the Student based on Student Id, so that TreeSet will store the Student object in sorted order based on Student id.

```
1.  public class TreeSetSortTest {
2.
3.    public static void main(String[] args) {
4.
5.        Student student1 = new Student(101, "Bob", "Atlanta");
6.        Student student2 = new Student(102, "Alex", "Lake
      Mary");
7.        Student student3 = new Student(103, "John", "Phoenix");
8.
9.        Set<Student> studentSet = new TreeSet<>();
10.       studentSet.add(student1);
11.       studentSet.add(student2);
12.       studentSet.add(student3);
13.
14.       for(Student s: studentSet) {
15.            System.out.println(s.toString());
16.        }
17.
18.    }
19.
20.  }
21.
22.  class Student implements Comparable<Student> {
23.
24.      private Integer id;
25.      private String name;
26.      private String address;
27.
28.      public Student(Integer id, String name, String address)
      {
29.            super();
30.            this.id = id;
31.            this.name = name;
32.            this.address = address;
33.      }
34.
35.      @Override
36.      public String toString() {
37.      return "Student [id=" + id + ", name=" + name + ",
      address=" + address + "]";
38.      }
39.
40.      @Override
41.      public int compareTo(Student o) {
42.            return this.id - o.id;
43.      }
```

106

```
Student [id=101, name=Bob, address=Atlanta]
Student [id=102, name=Alex, address=Lake Mary]
Student [id=103, name=John, address=Phoenix]
```

You can see it worked and sorted student object based on student id. Now let's say someone else is already using the Student class and you cannot modify the Student class to implement Comparable interface and force the Student object to compared based on student id. Or you do not have permission to modify the Student class. What you will do now? You can use Comparator interface. You can create a separate class that will implement Comparator to compare Student object. The advantage of Comparator is, you can have multiple Comparator to do comparisons in multiple way and you do not have to modify the actual class you are working on. See example below.

```
1. public class TreeSetSortTest {
2.
3.   public static void main(String[] args) {
4.
5.     Student student1 = new Student(101, "Bob", "Atlanta");
6.     Student student2 = new Student(102, "Alex", "Lake
   Mary");
7.     Student student3 = new Student(103, "John", "Phoenix");
8.
9.     // TreeSet using student id to sort
10.    Set<Student> studentIdSet = new TreeSet<>(new
   StudentIdComparator());
11.    studentIdSet.add(student1);
12.    studentIdSet.add(student2);
13.    studentIdSet.add(student3);
14.    System.out.println("Student sorted by id: ");
15.    for(Student s: studentIdSet) {
16.                    System.out.println(s.toString());
17.    }
18.
19.    // TreeSet using student id to sort
20.    Set<Student> studentNameSet = new TreeSet<>(new
   StudentNameComparator());
21.    studentNameSet.add(student1);
22.    studentNameSet.add(student2);
23.    studentNameSet.add(student3);
24.    System.out.println("");// new line
25.    System.out.println("Student sorted by name: ");
26.    for(Student s: studentNameSet) {
```

```
27.                          System.out.println(s.toString());
28.      }
29.    }
30.  }
31.
32.  class StudentIdComparator implements Comparator<Student> {
33.
34.    @Override
35.    public int compare(Student o1, Student o2) {
36.         return o1.id - o2.id;
37.    }
38.
39.  }
40.
41.  class StudentNameComparator implements Comparator<Student>
   {
42.
43.    @Override
44.    public int compare(Student o1, Student o2) {
45.         return o1.name.compareTo(o2.name);
46.    }
47.
48.  }
49.
50.  class Student{
51.
52.    Integer id;
53.    String name;
54.    String address;
55.
56.    public Student(Integer id, String name, String address)
   {
57.         super();
58.         this.id = id;
59.         this.name = name;
60.         this.address = address;
61.    }
62.
63.    @Override
64.    public String toString() {
65.         return "Student [id=" + id + ", name=" + name + ",
   address=" + address + "]";
66.  }
67.  }
```

Output:
```
Student sorted by id:
Student [id=101, name=Bob, address=Atlanta]
```

```
Student [id=102, name=Alex, address=Lake Mary]
Student [id=103, name=John, address=Phoenix]

Student sorted by name:
Student [id=102, name=Alex, address=Lake Mary]
Student [id=101, name=Bob, address=Atlanta]
Student [id=103, name=John, address=Phoenix]
```

In above example I have not touched the Student class. I have created two separate comparator class, one for Student id and one for student name.

How Set check for duplicate

Set do not allow duplicate elements, but how it checks for duplicate. Whenever you are using Integer, String, Long, Boolean, etc. it simply checks its value by using equals() methods. What will happen when we will use user defined object. Let's see below example.

```
1. public class SetTest {
2.
3.   public static void main(String[] args) {
4.
5.     Employee emp1 = new Employee(101, "John", "Atlanta");
6.     Employee emp2 = new Employee(101, "John", "Atlanta");
7.
8.     Set<Employee> empSet = new HashSet<>();
9.     empSet.add(emp1);
10.    empSet.add(emp2);
11.
12.    for(Employee emp: empSet) {
13.
14.                        System.out.println(emp.toString());
15.    }
16.  }
17.
18. }
19.
20. class Employee{
21.
22.   Integer id;
23.   String name;
24.   String address;
25.
26.   public Employee(Integer id, String name, String address) {
27.           super();
```

```
28.             this.id = id;
29.             this.name = name;
30.             this.address = address;
31.  }
32.
33.  @Override
34.  public String toString() {
35.             return "Employee [id=" + id + ", name=" + name +
    ", address=" + address + "]";
36.     }
37.  }
```

Output:
```
Employee [id=101, name=John, address=Atlanta]
Employee [id=101, name=John, address=Atlanta]
```

See the above example. Here Set don't know that both the employee is same. You are able to add both the object in Set even though all the values of both the objects are same.

What Set did in above example to eliminate duplicate? Set checked the Hashcode and equals methods of the object and found that both are different objects. So the solution is to override the hashCode() and equals() method into the Employee class. Now you want Set to work in a way that if employee id and name is same then both employees are same, irrespective of address. The simplest way to generate hashCode() and equals() using IDE and select only id and name variable to generate hashcode and equals method. You can do the custom implementation as well. In below example I am overriding hashCode(0 and equals() method and check if id and name is same then return true.

```
1. public class SetTest {
2.
3.   public static void main(String[] args) {
4.
5.      Employee emp1 = new Employee(101, "John", "Atlanta");
6.      Employee emp2 = new Employee(101, "John", "New York");
7.
8.      Set<Employee> empSet = new HashSet<>();
9.      empSet.add(emp1);
10.     empSet.add(emp2);
11.
12.     for(Employee emp: empSet) {
13.
14.                      System.out.println(emp.toString());
15.     }
16.   }
17.
```

```
18.  }
19.
20.  class Employee{
21.
22.     Integer id;
23.     String name;
24.     String address;
25.
26.     public Employee(Integer id, String name, String address)
     {
27.            super();
28.            this.id = id;
29.            this.name = name;
30.            this.address = address;
31.  }
32.
33.     @Override
34.     public int hashCode() {
35.            final int prime = 31;
36.            int result = 1;
37.            result = prime * result + ((id == null) ? 0 :
   id.hashCode());
38.            result = prime * result + ((name == null) ? 0 :
   name.hashCode());
39.            return result;
40.  }
41.
42.     @Override
43.     public boolean equals(Object obj) {
44.            if (this == obj)
45.                   return true;
46.            if (obj == null)
47.                   return false;
48.            if (getClass() != obj.getClass())
49.                   return false;
50.            Employee other = (Employee) obj;
51.            if (id == null) {
52.                   if (other.id != null)
53.                          return false;
54.            } else if (!id.equals(other.id))
55.                   return false;
56.            if (name == null) {
57.                   if (other.name != null)
58.                          return false;
59.            } else if (!name.equals(other.name))
60.                   return false;
61.            return true;
62.  }
63.
```

```
64.    @Override
65.    public String toString() {
66.           return "Employee [id=" + id + ", name=" + name +
       ", address=" + address + "]";
67.      }
68.    }
```

Output:
```
Employee [id=101, name=John, address=Atlanta]
```

In above example, Set checks for equality. It checks for hashCode() and found that hashcode of both the object is same. Then it checks equals() method and it returned true, means both objects are same and it ignores the second insertion. Here hashCode() and equals() are implemented to check equality based on id and name only that is why even though the address in both of objects are different, it is considering the same employee.

Queue Interface

Queue stores element in order that can be retrieved in FIFO order. Queue is implemented through LinkedList and PriorityQueue class. LinkedList implementation of queue maintains the FIFO ordering. Priority queue does not guarantee FIFO, it will be FIFO but order can be changed based on priority. Queue provides add(), remove(), peek(), poll(), size(), and contains() methods.

LinkedList

LinkedList implementation of Queue provides the FIFO implementation. You can see in below example with all the methods.

```
1. public class LinkedListQueueTest {
2.
3.   public static void main(String[] args) {
4.
5.     Queue<String> colors = new LinkedList<>();
6.     colors.add("White");
7.     colors.add("Blue");
8.     colors.add("Yellow");
9.     colors.add("Green");
10.    colors.add("Red");
11.
12.    //print all colors
```

```
13.     System.out.println("All colors: "+colors);
14.
15.     //get head of the queue without removing from queue
16.     String headElement = colors.peek(); // White as FIFO
17.     System.out.println("Head of the queue is:
   "+headElement);
18.
19.     //get head of the queue and remove from queue
20.     String headElement1 = colors.poll(); // White as FIFO
21.     System.out.println("Head of the queue is:
   "+headElement1);
22.
23.     //get head of the queue again without removing from
   queue
24.     String headElement3 = colors.peek(); // Blue as FIFO
25.     System.out.println("Head of the queue now is:
   "+headElement3);
26.
27.     colors.remove(); // removed from top as FIFO- removed
   Blue
28.
29.     //get head of the queue again
30.     String headElement4 = colors.peek(); // Yellow as FIFO
31.     System.out.println("Head of the queue now is:
   "+headElement4);
32.
33.     //print all colors
34.     System.out.println("remaining colors: "+colors);
35.
36.     //Size of colors
37.     System.out.println("Number of colors in queue: "+
   colors.size());
38.
39.     }
40.  }
```

Output:
```
All colors: [White, Blue, Yellow, Green, Red]
Head of the queue is: White
Head of the queue is: White
Head of the queue now is: Blue
Head of the queue now is: Yellow
remaining colors: [Yellow, Green, Red]
Number of colors in queue: 3
```

In the above example you can see LinkedList implementation of Queue is having good support of FIFO.

PriorityQueue

PriorityQueue is the implementation of Queue provides FIFO support, but FIFO based retrieval can be changed based on priority. To set the priority PriorityQueue compare the value of elements. If values cannot be compared, then you cannot use it in PriorityQueue. Similar to the TreeSet, your class has to implement comparable interface, or you need to create comparable class similarly we used for TreeSet, if you want to store your class object in PriorityQueue. Below is the example.

```
1.  public class PriorityQueueTest {
2.
3.    public static void main(String[] args) {
4.
5.        Stud student1 = new Stud(102, "Alex", "Lake Mary");
6.        Stud student2 = new Stud(101, "Bob", "Atlanta");
7.        Stud student3 = new Stud(103, "John", "Phoenix");
8.
9.        // TreeSet using student id to sort
10.       Queue<Stud> studentIdQ = new PriorityQueue<>();
11.       studentIdQ.add(student1);
12.       studentIdQ.add(student2);
13.       studentIdQ.add(student3);
14.       System.out.println("Student sorted by id: ");
15.
16.       System.out.println(studentIdQ.poll());
17.       System.out.println(studentIdQ.poll());
18.       System.out.println(studentIdQ.poll());
19.
20.   }
21. }
22.
23. class Stud implements Comparable<Stud>{
24.
25.     Integer id;
26.     String name;
27.     String address;
28.
29.     public Stud(Integer id, String name, String address) {
30.         super();
31.         this.id = id;
32.         this.name = name;
33.         this.address = address;
34.     }
35.
36.     @Override
37.     public String toString() {
```

```
38.            return "Stud [id=" + id + ", name=" + name + ",
   address=" + address + "]";
39.     }
40.
41.    @Override
42.    public int compareTo(Stud o) {
43.            return 1;
44.     }
45.  }
```

Output:
```
Stud [id=102, name=Alex, address=Lake Mary]
Stud [id=101, name=Bob, address=Atlanta]
Stud [id=103, name=John, address=Phoenix]
```

In above code you can see I am returning 1 from compareTo() method in every case, and PriorityQueue works fine as FIFO ordering. Now see the below example.

```
1. public class PriorityQueueTest {
2.
3.   public static void main(String[] args) {
4.
5.      Stud student1 = new Stud(102, "Alex", "Lake Mary");
6.      Stud student2 = new Stud(101, "Bob", "Atlanta");
7.      Stud student3 = new Stud(103, "John", "Phoenix");
8.
9.      // TreeSet using student id to sort
10.     Queue<Stud> studentIdQ = new PriorityQueue<>();
11.     studentIdQ.add(student1);
12.     studentIdQ.add(student2);
13.     studentIdQ.add(student3);
14.     System.out.println("Student sorted by id: ");
15.
16.     System.out.println(studentIdQ.poll());
17.     System.out.println(studentIdQ.poll());
18.     System.out.println(studentIdQ.poll());
19.
20.    }
21.  }
22.
23.  class Stud implements Comparable<Stud>{
24.
25.     Integer id;
26.     String name;
27.     String address;
28.
29.     public Stud(Integer id, String name, String address) {
```

```
30.          super();
31.          this.id = id;
32.          this.name = name;
33.          this.address = address;
34.      }
35.
36.    @Override
37.    public String toString() {
38.      return "Stud [id=" + id + ", name=" + name + ",
   address=" + address + "]";
39.      }
40.
41.    @Override
42.    public int compareTo(Stud o) {
43.          return this.id - o.id;
44.      }
45.  }
```

Output:
```
Stud [id=101, name=Bob, address=Atlanta]
Stud [id=102, name=Alex, address=Lake Mary]
Stud [id=103, name=John, address=Phoenix]
```

In above example you can see PriorityQueue is not following FIFO ordering and ordering gets changed based on priority (here priority is based on id being set in compareTo() method).

Deque Interface

Deque double ended queue in which you can insert and retrieve elements from both sides. Deque operations are similar to the queue with support of addition and removal of elements from both sides. Deque can be implemented as queue by implementing FIFO (First-in-first-out), and it can be also implemented like stack by implementing LIFO (Last-in-first-out). LinkedList and ArrayDeque provides implementation of Deque interface.

Map Interface

Map can store key-value pair data. Map interface do not extend the Collection interface. In Map every key is associated with at most one value. For a given key you can find value in map in constant time. You cannot have duplicate key in Map. A map contains a set of keys, collection of values, and key-value mapping. A map implementation class could be HashMap, LinkedHashMap, or TreeMap.

HashMap

A HashMap is very close to the HashTable. HashMap implements Map interface and provides all the functionality of Map. HashMap accepts only unique key and cannot contains duplicate key. HashMap can contains maximum of one null value as key, but it may contain many null values. HashMap does not guarantee the order of elements it stores. The initial capacity of HashMap is 16 with load factor of 0.75. What is initial capacity and what is load factor? Initial capacity is the capacity when HashMap gets created. Load factor is measure of percentage of HashMap gets full then its capacity will get increased automatically. That means when the number of entries exceeds the product of capacity and load factor then it gets re-hashed and increased the capacity. HashMap is not synchronized and not made for using in concurrent situation. If multiple threads are going to use the HashMap then you can wrapped your HashMap with syncronizedMap() method like below at the time of map creation.

```
Map m = Collections.synchronizedMap(new HashMap(...));
```

If the HashMap is being modified in threads in multithreading environment, then it may throw ConcurrentModificationException.

```
1. public class HashMapTest {
2.
3.   public static void main(String[] args)
4.   {
5.     // Create HashMap
6.     Map<Integer, String> map = new HashMap<>();
7.
8.     // Add elements
9.     map.put(101, "Red");
10.    map.put(102, "Blue");
11.    map.put(103, "Green");
12.
13.    //print size
14.    System.out.println("Map Size: "+map.size());
15.    System.out.println("");//new line
16.    //Check if key is there
17.    if (map.containsKey(102)) {
18.      String val = map.get(102);
19.      System.out.println("value for 102 is: "+ val);
```

```
20.    }
21.    System.out.println("");//new line
22.    //Iterate for key-value
23.    System.out.println("Printing key-value:");
24.    for (Map.Entry<Integer, String> e : map.entrySet()) {
25.      System.out.println(e.getKey() + " - " + e.getValue());
26.     }
27.    }
28. }
```

Output:
```
Map Size: 3

value for 102 is: Blue

Printing key-value:
101 - Red
102 - Blue
103 - Green
```

Why does not allow duplicate key

Map does not allow duplicate key. The reason the same why Set does not allow the duplicate elements. Map stores its key in set. If you call `map.entrySet()` then it will return the Set of keys. You already know Set does not allow duplicate values. How set compares the duplicate elements with hashCode() and equals() method is already explained in Set section. Please go through that.

LinkedHashMap

LinkedHashMap is the implementation of HashTable and LinkedList with the implementation of Map interface. It maintains a doubly linked list. It maintains the order of insertion, means the order key is inserted into the LinkedHashMap. HashMap is quicker than LinkedHashMap for insertion, find, and deletion operation. If you do not require to maintain the order of insertion, then HashMap is better choice.

```
1. public class LinkedHashMapTest {
2.
3.   public static void main(String[] args) {
4.
5.     Map<Integer, String> map = new LinkedHashMap<>();
6.
7.     // Add elements
8.     map.put(101, "Red");
```

```
9.      map.put(103, "Green");
10.     map.put(102, "Blue");
11.
12.     //print map
13.     System.out.println(map);
14.
15.     //change the value
16.     map.put(101, "Yellow");
17.
18.     //print again
19.     System.out.println(map);
20.
21.     //remove Green
22.     map.remove(103);
23.
24.     //print again
25.     System.out.println(map);
26.
27.     //iterate and print the map
28.     System.out.println("Iterate and Print map: ");
29.     for (Map.Entry<Integer, String> mapElement :
   map.entrySet()) {
30.
31.         //get key
32.         int key = (int)mapElement.getKey();
33.
34.         // Find value
35.         String value = (String)mapElement.getValue();
36.
37.         //print key-value pair
38.         System.out.println(key + " - " + value);
39.         }
40.
41.     }
42.
43. }
```

Output:
```
{101=Red, 103=Green, 102=Blue}
{101=Yellow, 103=Green, 102=Blue}
{101=Yellow, 102=Blue}
Iterate and Print map:
101 - Yellow
102 - Blue
```

Above example shows how LinkedHashMap maintains the order of insertion even though you modify or remove the elements.

TreeMap

TreeMap is the implementation of red-black tree. TreeMap sorts its keys based on natural ordering of key or the comparator provided at the time of creation. You can also implement Comparable interface to your class you are going to use as key of TreeMap. TreeMap key sorting is similar to the TreeSet. TreeMap is also not synchronized and you can use synchronizedSortedMap() method at the creation time to use map in multithreading environment.

```
1.  public class TreeMapTest {
2.
3.    public static void main(String[] args) {
4.
5.        //natural ordering
6.        Map<Integer, String> map = new TreeMap<>();
7.        map.put(51, "John");
8.        map.put(31, "Alex");
9.        System.out.println(map);
10.
11.       //create user defined object for key
12.       ColorTest color1 = new ColorTest(105, "Green");
13.       ColorTest color2 = new ColorTest(103, "Blue");
14.       ColorTest color4 = new ColorTest(102, "Orange");
15.
16.       // Sort by Color id
17.       Map<ColorTest, String> map1 = new TreeMap<>(new
   ColorTestIdComparator());
18.       map1.put(color1, "Wall color");
19.       map1.put(color2, "Roof color");
20.       map1.put(color4, "Kitchen color");
21.
22.       //print map
23.       System.out.println(map1);
24.
25.       // Sort by Color name
26.       Map<ColorTest, String> map2 = new TreeMap<>(new
   ColorTestNameComparator());
27.       map2.put(color1, "Wall color");
28.       map2.put(color2, "Roof color");
29.       map2.put(color4, "Kitchen color");
30.
31.       //print map
32.       System.out.println(map2);
33.
34.    }
35.
```

```
36.    }
37.
38.    class ColorTestIdComparator implements
       Comparator<ColorTest> {
39.
40.        @Override
41.        public int compare(ColorTest o1, ColorTest o2) {
42.            return o1.id - o2.id;
43.        }
44.
45.    }
46.
47.    class ColorTestNameComparator implements
       Comparator<ColorTest> {
48.
49.        @Override
50.        public int compare(ColorTest o1, ColorTest o2) {
51.            return o1.name.compareTo(o2.name);
52.        }
53.
54.    }
55.
56.    class ColorTest{
57.
58.        Integer id;
59.        String name;
60.
61.        public ColorTest(Integer id, String name) {
62.            super();
63.            this.id = id;
64.            this.name = name;
65.        }
66.
67.        @Override
68.        public String toString() {
69.            return "ColorTest [id=" + id + ", name=" + name +
       "]";
70.        }
71.    }
```

Output:
```
{31=Alex, 51=John}
{ColorTest [id=102, name=Orange]=Kitchen color, ColorTest
[id=103, name=Blue]=Roof color, ColorTest [id=105,
name=Green]=Wall color}
```

```
{ColorTest [id=103, name=Blue]=Roof color, ColorTest [id=105,
name=Green]=Wall color, ColorTest [id=102, name=Orange]=Kitchen
color}
```

Above example explains working of TreeMap. TreeMap's keys are stored like TreeSet. You can see the sorting of key works similar to the TreeSet.

6   Multithreading

Multithreading in java is about concurrency, you can run your program concurrently. You have one method for some operation, you want your method runs simultaneously for different section of dataset.

When you are talking about programs or application, you are talking about process. A process has its own memory space. A process has a self-contained execution environment. A process has a complete, private set of basic run-time environment.

A thread is a lightweight process. A thread is a process in execution in a program. JVM allows an application to have multiple threads of execution running concurrently. Each thread has a priority. Threads with higher priority are executed in preference to the threads with lower priority.

Every java application has a default main thread that starts with the execution of main() method. From this main thread you can fork multiple thread to execute your functions concurrently. For each thread you will create, JVM provides separate memory stacks to every thread, so the threads do not interfere each other. But still there are common area or common data threads can share, and you have to make sure that threads are not stepping on each other while using common area or common data, and threads should use this common area or data in synchronized manner.

Java provides built-in libraries to create and manage thread. You can create thread by extending Thread class or by implementing runnable interface.

Java do not support multiple inheritance, if your class is already extending some other class you cannot extend thread class, you will have only choice to implement runnable interface. Once you extend Thread class you cannot extend any other class in future if needed. Because of these reasons implementing runnable interface become better choice to create thread.

If you see the Thread class provided by java is itself implementing runnable interface.

Thread Class

You can create new thread by creating subclass of Thread class, and subclass should override run method of Thread class. Instance of your subclass can be allocated and started. See the example below.

```
1. public class PrimeThreadTest {
2.
3.   public static void main(String[] args) {
4.
5.     // List of 5 numbers
6.     List<Integer> numList = Arrays.asList(101, 201, 301,
   401, 501);
7.
8.     // Creates 5 thread, all thread calculate prime number
   concurrently
9.     for(Integer i : numList) {
10.         PrimeThread p = new PrimeThread(i);
11.         p.start();
12.     }
13.   }
14. }
15. // Thread subclass
16. class PrimeThread extends Thread {
```

```
17.
18.     int minPrime;
19.
20.     PrimeThread(int minPrime) {
21.             this.minPrime = minPrime;
22.     }
23.
24.     // thread execute this method
25.     @Override
26.     public void run() {
27.     System.out.println("Started Thread id:
   "+this.currentThread().getId() + " at:
   "+LocalDateTime.now());
28.     int nextPrime = nextPrime(this.minPrime);
29.     System.out.println(nextPrime);
30.     System.out.println("Finished Thread id:
   "+this.currentThread().getId() + " at:
   "+LocalDateTime.now());
31.     }
32.
33.     int nextPrime(int N)
34.     {
35.         if (N <= 1)
36.             return 2;
37.
38.         int prime = N;
39.         boolean found = false;
40.
41.         while (!found)
42.         {
43.             prime++;
44.
45.             if (isPrime(prime))
46.                 found = true;
47.         }
48.
49.         return prime;
50.     }
51.
52.     boolean isPrime(int n)
53.     {
54.         if (n <= 1) return false;
55.         if (n <= 3) return true;
56.
57.         if (n % 2 == 0 || n % 3 == 0) return false;
58.
59.         for (int i = 5; i * i <= n; i = i + 6)
60.             if (n % i == 0 || n % (i + 2) == 0)
61.                 return false;
```

```
62.
63.        return true;
64.    }
65. }
```

Output:
```
Started Thread id: 15 at: 2020-07-07T19:26:48.983213
Started Thread id: 14 at: 2020-07-07T19:26:48.983183
Started Thread id: 16 at: 2020-07-07T19:26:48.983165
Started Thread id: 13 at: 2020-07-07T19:26:48.982979
Started Thread id: 12 at: 2020-07-07T19:26:48.983163
211
103
503
307
Finished Thread id: 12 at: 2020-07-07T19:26:48.986437
409
Finished Thread id: 16 at: 2020-07-07T19:26:48.986501
Finished Thread id: 14 at: 2020-07-07T19:26:48.986501
Finished Thread id: 15 at: 2020-07-07T19:26:48.986623
Finished Thread id: 13 at: 2020-07-07T19:26:48.986428
```

In above example 5 threads gets created in loop and each thread called method to calculates the next prime number for a number and print the result. Here you can see that start() method cause to create thread by runtime system and schedule it for execution, which executes threads run() method. As you see here a unique thread id gets allocated to each thread. In above code example sequence of execution of thread is not guaranteed.

Runnable Interface

You can create a thread by implementing Runnable interface and overriding of run() method. This is the better way to create thread than creating thread by extending Thread class. To use the Runnable interface, you need to create a class that will implement the Runnable interface and implements the run() method. Then you can pass the class instance into Thread constructor and call start() method on it. See below the same example of calculating Prime number we have implemented for Thread class.

```
1. public class PrimeThreadTest {
2.
3.    public static void main(String[] args) {
4.
5.      // List of 5 numbers
```

```
6.      List<Integer> numList = Arrays.asList(101, 201, 301,
   401, 501);
7.
8.      // Creates 5 thread, all thread calculate prime number
   concurrently
9.      for(Integer i : numList) {
10.     //Instantiate PrimeThread class and pass as an argument
11.     Thread p = new Thread(new PrimeThread(i));
12.          p.start();
13.      }
14.    }
15.  }
16.  // Thread subclass
17.  class PrimeThread implements Runnable {
18.
19.     int minPrime;
20.
21.     PrimeThread(int minPrime) {
22.          this.minPrime = minPrime;
23.      }
24.
25.     // thread execute this method
26.     @Override
27.     public void run() {
28.     System.out.println("Started Thread id:
   "+Thread.currentThread().getId() + " at:
   "+LocalDateTime.now());
29.     int nextPrime = nextPrime(this.minPrime);
30.     System.out.println(nextPrime);
31.     System.out.println("Finished Thread id:
   "+Thread.currentThread().getId() + " at:
   "+LocalDateTime.now());
32.      }
33.
34.   int nextPrime(int N)
35.   {
36.      if (N <= 1)
37.          return 2;
38.
39.      int prime = N;
40.      boolean found = false;
41.
42.      while (!found)
43.      {
44.          prime++;
45.
46.          if (isPrime(prime))
47.              found = true;
48.      }
```

```
49.
50.      return prime;
51.  }
52.
53.  boolean isPrime(int n)
54.  {
55.      if (n <= 1) return false;
56.      if (n <= 3) return true;
57.
58.      if (n % 2 == 0 || n % 3 == 0) return false;
59.
60.      for (int i = 5; i * i <= n; i = i + 6)
61.          if (n % i == 0 || n % (i + 2) == 0)
62.          return false;
63.
64.      return true;
65.    }
66.
67.  }
```

Output:
```
Started Thread id: 14 at: 2020-07-08T14:28:12.220123
307
Finished Thread id: 14 at: 2020-07-08T14:28:12.220935
Started Thread id: 12 at: 2020-07-08T14:28:12.220102
Started Thread id: 15 at: 2020-07-08T14:28:12.218202
Started Thread id: 16 at: 2020-07-08T14:28:12.219283
503
Finished Thread id: 16 at: 2020-07-08T14:28:12.221824
103
Started Thread id: 13 at: 2020-07-08T14:28:12.220063
211
Finished Thread id: 12 at: 2020-07-08T14:28:12.222011
409
Finished Thread id: 13 at: 2020-07-08T14:28:12.222061
Finished Thread id: 15 at: 2020-07-08T14:28:12.222142
```

Above example works similar to the extending of Thread class.

Thread Properties

Each thread has some attributes. Based on these attributes you can identify the threads, knows the thread status, or control the thread priority. Below are the thread attributes.

- Thread Id: Thread id is a unique identifier for each thread. When thread gets created one unique id gets assigned to the thread.

- Thread Name: This attribute stores the name of the thread. Thread name can be set at the time of thread creation like below.

```
1.  // List of 5 numbers
2.  List<Integer> numList = Arrays.asList(101, 201, 301, 401,
    501);
3.
4.  // Creates 5 thread, all thread calculate prime number
    concurrently
5.  for(Integer i : numList) {
6.     //Instantiate PrimeThread class and pass as an argument
7.     Thread p = new Thread(new PrimeThread(i));
8.      //setr name of the thread
9.     p.setName("PrimeThread"+i);
10.          p.start();
11.  }
```

- Thread Priority: Changing thread priority is not recommended. If you set the thread priority there is a possibility that higher priority thread will get scheduled with higher priority by operating system, but there is no guarantee. Thread priority can be between 1 to 10, 1 (MIN_PRIORITY) is the minimum and 10 (MAX_PRIORITY) is maximum. By default thread created with priority 5 (NORM_PRIORITY).

```
1.  Thread p = new Thread(new PrimeThread(i));
2.
3.  //set the thread priority
4.  p.setPriority(Thread.MAX_PRIORITY); //10
5.
6.  p.start(); // start the thrtead
```

- Thread Status: State attribute of thread stores the state of thread. The thread can have one of the six state defined in the Thread.State enum. Thread.State Enum is defined as below.

```
1.      public enum State {
2.          NEW,
3.          RUNNABLE,
4.          BLOCKED,
5.          WAITING,
6.          TIMED_WAITING,
7.          TERMINATED;
8.      }
```

You can check thread status as-

```
1.    @Override
2.    public void run() {
3.        State st = Thread.currentThread().getState();
4.        System.out.println(st);
5.    }
```

All the six thread states are defined as below.

NEW: A thread that is not yet started.

RUNNABLE: A thread in the runnable state is executing in the JVM but it may be waiting for other resources from the operating system like processor.

BLOCKED: A thread is in the blocked state waiting for a monitor lock to enter a synchronized block/method after calling Object.wait() method.

WAITING: A thread is in waiting state is waiting for another thread to perform a particular action. A thread that has called Object.wait() without timeout on an object is waiting for another thread to call Object.notify() or Object.notifyAll() on that object. A thread has called Thread.join() is waiting for specified thread to terminate.

TIMED_WAITING: Thread state for a waiting thread with a specified waiting time. A thread is in the timed waiting state due to the call of Thtread.sleep(ling timeout), or Object.wait(long timeout) with a timeout, or Thread.join() with a timeout.

TERMINATED: A thread has completed execution is in terminated state.

Thread Lifecycle

Thread lifecycle is nothing but how thread changes its state. All thread started with NEW state, and then move to RUNNABLE state. After RUNNABLE state thread either starts RUNNING or moved to BLOCKED or WAITING state. RUNNING is not a defined state, but you can say if thread crossed the RUNNABLE state and not in BLOCKED, WAITING, TIMED_WAITING, or TERMINATED state, then thread is in RUNNING state. You can see below image to understand thread states lifecycle.

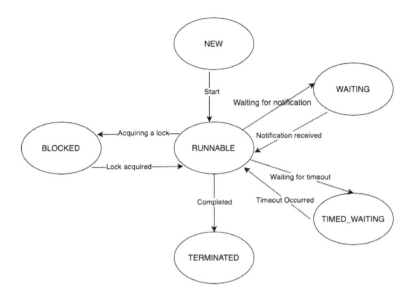

Thread Synchronization

When two or more thread trying to access the same resource then you need to use thread synchronization to ensure that one thread at a time can use that resource. If you allow multiple thread to use a method, or use a section of code, or a shared data, you must ensure that the race condition should not happen. To avoid race condition, you can properly synchronize those shared resources.

Thread synchronization comes with the concept of monitor. Monitor is an object that can be owned by one thread at a time. In the process of synchronization when the thread acquires the lock that means it entered the monitor and monitor is locked by the thread. Other thread is trying to enter the monitor will be waiting for the monitor to free.

You can synchronize the thread in two ways, either by synchronizing the method or by using synchronized block.

Race condition

Race condition occurs when two or more thread access shared data and they try to change it at same time and produce unexpected results. Race condition can be avoided by proper thread synchronization.

Synchronized method

You can synchronize the whole method to make it thread safe. This is the easiest way of synchronization; you just need to add synchronized keyword in method as below.

```
1. public class SyncronizationTest {
2.
3.   public static void main(String[] args) {
4.
5.     TestThread tt = new TestThread();
6.
7.     for(int i=0; i<3; i++) {
8.
9.             Thread t = new Thread(tt);
10.                   t.start();
11.          }
12.   }
13.
14. }
15.
16. class TestThread implements Runnable {
17.
18.    private int value = 0;
19.
20.    @Override
21.    public void run() {
22.    //gets call in thread
23.    incrementValue();
24.    System.out.println(getValue());
25.    }
26.
27.    public int getValue() {
28.          return value;
29.    }
30.
31.    //synchronized method
32.    public synchronized void incrementValue() {
33.          value++;
34.    }
35. }
```

Output:
1
3
2

In above example, we are synchronizing the incrementValue() method. Here order of above output is not constant, it may vary and there is no guarantee of sequence of execution. As first thread entered to the monitor of synchronized method while second and third thread is waiting. After monitor gets freed, there is no guarantee which among the second or third thread will get the monitor. You can run above program multiple time and see the sequence of number in output may vary.

As we have synchronized method, can we have synchronized constructor? The answer is no. If you use synchronized keyword with constructor, then it will give you error. Constructor cannot be synchronized, because constructor gets called at the time of creating threads, when you create an object to pass to the thread class constructor.

Synchronized Blocks

There is a situation when synchronizing the whole method is not required, you may need to synchronize part of method, or few lines inside the method. In those situations, you can use synchronized blocks. Synchronizations use Intrinsic locks. Let's see what it is.

Intrinsic lock is same as monitor lock. When you lock section of code or a method using synchronized block then it acquires Intrinsic lock over the object and release the lock once it's done the processing. Once a thread acquires a lock on object the other threads are block using any synchronized method or any synchronized block using the same object. Once a thread acquires the lock it can call other methods on that object without acquiring the lock again. **If you are using synchronized keyword in static method, then you do not need object to call those methods. In this case of static method Intrinsic lock will get applied on whole class level**.

Now let's talk about synchronized block. In synchronized block you need an object to apply lock on. Below is the example of synchronized block.

```
1.    public void multipleTransactions() {
2.        int dollerValue = 50;
3.        // lots of code here that do not need to
      synchronized
4.
5.
6.        //code that needs to synchronized
7.        // synchronized block
8.        synchronized(this) {
9.            dollerValue = dollerValue+ 100;
10.       }
11.  }
```

In above code I am providing this object (current object) to the intrinsic lock to control access of synchronized block.

You may need to synchronize multiple section of code inside a method. If those multiple sections are unrelated and do not need to synchronize at the same time, you can use multiple objects to synchronize those blocks. Let's see an example below.

```
1. Object o1 = new Object();
2. Object o2 = new Object();
3.
4. public void multipleTransactions() {
5.     int dollerValue = 50;
6.     int otherValue = 75;
7.     // lots of code here that do not need to synchronized
8.
9.     //code that needs to synchronized
10.    // synchronized block
11.    synchronized(o1) {
12.            dollerValue = dollerValue+ 100;
13.    }
14.
15.    // synchronized block
16.    synchronized(o2) {
17.            otherValue = otherValue+ 100;
18.     }
19.  }
```

In above example the two synchronized blocks, if a thread entered into first synchronized block at the same time another thread can enter into the second synchronized block as both blocks are locking on different objects.

Volatile

Volatile variable reduces the risk of consistency errors. Changes in volatile variable can be seen by other threads. Let's say some thread is changing the value of volatile and some threads are reading the value, the threads changing or reading the values of volatile will always see the latest value of it.

Liveness problems

Multiple threads execute the programs in timely manners is called liveness. Threads can take turns to get access of common resources if needed. The section of code protected by using lock, is called critical section in java. The common liveness problems are deadlock, starvation, and livelock.

Deadlock

Deadlock is a situation where two or more threads are blocked forever and waiting for each other to release. Below example may get into deadlock waiting for each other.

```
1. public class DeadlockTest {
2.
3.   static class DeadlockGenerator{
4.
5.     private final String objName;
6.
7.     public DeadlockGenerator(String objName) {
8.          this.objName = objName;
9.     }
10.
11.    public String getObjName() {
12.         return this.objName;
13.    }
14.
15.    public synchronized void outer(DeadlockGenerator obj) {
16.       System.out.println("In outer with "+ this.objName+ ",
   and :" + obj.getObjName());
17.       obj.inner(this);
18.       try {
19.               Thread.sleep(1000);
20.          } catch (InterruptedException e) {
21.             // TODO Auto-generated catch block
22.             e.printStackTrace();
23.          }
24.
25.    }
26.
27.    public synchronized void inner(DeadlockGenerator obj) {
28.       System.out.println("In Inner with "+ this.objName+ ",
   and :" + obj.getObjName());
29.       }
30.    }
31.
32.    public static void main(String[] args) {
33.
34.    final DeadlockGenerator objOne = new
   DeadlockGenerator("objOne");
```

```
35.    final DeadlockGenerator objTwo = new
  DeadlockGenerator("objTwo");
36.
37.    //create thread using anonymous inner class
38.    new Thread(new Runnable() {
39.
40.    @Override
41.    public void run() {
42.         objOne.outer(objTwo);
43.
44.    }
45.  }).start();;
46.
47.   //create thread using anonymous inner class
48.    new Thread(new Runnable() {
49.
50.        @Override
51.        public void run() {
52.             objTwo.outer(objOne);
53.
54.        }
55.    }).start();;
56.
57.    }
58.
59.  }
```

Above code may get into deadlock anytime. Thread A is locked on objB and waiting for objA and thread B is locked on objA and waiting for objB, in that way both threads kept waiting for each other.

Starvation

Starvation is a situation where deadlock occurs but get resolved after some time. Here in this case waiting time is not infinite, after some interval of time, waiting threads will always get the resource for which it is waiting for.

Livelock

Livelock is a situation when threads are busy to respond each other to resume work. Livelock is like a deadlock where thread is unable to make progress, but they are not locked, meaning they are not in the waiting state. Thread t1 holds the resource r1 and sending message to the thread t2 to release the resource r2, while thread t2 can not release the resource until it gets the resource r1, so thread t2 is keep sending message to thread t1 to release the resource r1. Thread t1 is in the same situation, and it cannot release the resource r1 until it gets the resource r2. This creates a kind of loop where threads t1 and t2 keep communicating to each other for resource, and they are not able to proceed.

Executors

Executor interface provides a single method execute(). Executor creates threads in a similar way you create thread using Runnable interface. Executors provide more capability to manage the thread. You can use Runnable or Callable tasks with executor and also it manages thread pool automatically. I will explain the difference between Runnable and Callable first. As we already talked about Runnable interface, that has run() method to start (schedule) the thread. Callable is similar to the Runnable, with two major difference. Callable has call() method similar to Runnable has run() method. Callable call() method may return the value in the form of future object.

Callable example

```
1.  public class CallableTest implements Callable<String>
2.  {
3.    // call method returns String
4.    @Override
5.    public String call() throws Exception {
6.          return Thread.currentThread().getName();
7.    }
8.
9.
10. public static void main(String[] args) throws Exception
11.  {
12.    //callable class object
13.    Callable<String> callable = new CallableTest();
14.
15.    //Future task
16.    FutureTask<String> futureTask = new
    FutureTask<>(callable);
17.
18.    // thread object accept future task object as an
    argument
19.    Thread t = new Thread(futureTask);
20.
21.    // Schedule thread
22.    t.start();
23.
```

```
24.     // Wait until thread is finished to get return
25.     String threadReturn = futureTask.get();
26.
27.     System.out.println("Thread name is: "+ threadReturn);
28.   }
29.
30.
31.   }
```

In above code example, Callable interface is being used to created and schedule thread. Callable provides call() method that can return the values. You can get return values using blocking get() method. The get() method provided by future is blocking method, blocking method means it will wait at the same point where you call the get() method, until all the thread scheduled is finished and return value of call() method is available.

Executor interface

Executor interface decouples task submission from how the task will run. The executors are used in place of explicitly creating thread. Executor interface supports launching new task. ExecutorService interface extends from executor interface provided extra feature to manage lifecycle of thread. Again, ScheduledExecutorService interface extends ExecutorService interface that provides more features on top of ExecutorService interface like Future execution of task or periodic execution of tasks.
Below is the example of Executor interface.

```
1. public class ExecutorTest implements Executor{
2.
3.   public static void main(String[] args) {
4.
5.     //Executor object
6.     ExecutorTest e = new ExecutorTest();
7.
8.     //Schedule thread
9.     e.execute(new MyThread());
10.   }
11.
12.   //Executors Execute method
13.   @Override
14.   public void execute(Runnable command) {
15.
16.         new Thread(command).start();
17.
18.   }
```

```
19.
20.   }
21.
22.   //Thread class extending Runnable
23.   class MyThread implements Runnable {
24.
25.      //Runnable's run method
26.      @Override
27.      public void run() {
28.
29.         System.out.println("MyThread is running.");
30.
31.      }
32.
33.   }
```

In above example, Executor's execute() method triggers the thread created using Runnable.

ExecutorService interface

ExecutorService interface extends Executor interface. ExecutorService interface provides execute() method as it extends Executor interface, it also provides submit() method that accepts Runnable objects.

ExecutorService can be shutdown, which will cause to reject new tasks. It provides two different method for shutdown, shutdown() and shutdownNow(). The shutdown() method allow previously submitted task to execute before terminating. The shutdownNow() prevents waiting task from starting and attempts to stops currently executing tasks. Upon termination, the executor will have no tasks actively executing, awaiting execution, and no new tasks can be submitted.

The ExecutorService's submit method extends the base method execute by creating and returning a Future that can be used to cancel execution or wait for completion. The method invokeAny() and invokeAll() can execute a collection of tasks and then waiting for at least one or all to complete. The class ExecutorCompletionService can be used to write customized version of these methods.

The Executors class provides the factory method for ExecutorService. Below is the example of executor service interface using runnable interface for creating threads.

```
1. public class ExecutorServiceRunnableTest {
2.
3.    void methodExecInThread(){
```

```
4.
5.      try {
6.            Thread.sleep(5000);
7.      } catch (InterruptedException ex) {
8.            ex.printStackTrace();
9.      }
10.     }
11.
12.     public void executorServiceExecuteExample() throws
    InterruptedException{
13.
14.     //Creates a thread pool that reuses a fixed number of
    threads
15.       ExecutorService executorService =
    Executors.newFixedThreadPool(2);
16.
17.       try{
18.
19.         executorService.execute(new Runnable() {
20.
21.           @Override
22.           public void run() {
23.
    System.out.println("Running " +
    Thread.currentThread().getName());
24.
    methodExecInThread();
25.
26.             }
27.         });
28.
29.       //ExecutorService execute() method
30.       executorService.execute(new Runnable() {
31.
32.           @Override
33.           public void run() {
34.
    System.out.println("Running " +
    Thread.currentThread().getName());
35.
    methodExecInThread();
36.
37.             }
38.         });
39.
40.
41.       }
42.       finally{
```

```
43.         //Initiates an orderly shutdown in which previously
     submitted
44.         //tasks are executed, but no new tasks will be
     accepted.
45.         executorService.shutdown();
46.
47.         /* Blocks until all tasks have completed execution
     after a shutdown
48.          * request, or the timeout occurs, or the current
     thread is
49.          * interrupted, whichever happens first.*/
50.                         executorService.awaitTermination(3,
     TimeUnit.SECONDS);
51.      }
52.    }
53.
54.    public void executorServiceSubmitExample() throws
     InterruptedException{
55.
56.    //Creates a thread pool that reuses a fixed number of
     threads
57.    ExecutorService executorService =
     Executors.newFixedThreadPool(2);
58.
59.    try{
60.
61.      //ExecutorService submit() method
62.      Future<?> task1Future = executorService.submit(new
     Runnable() {
63.
64.         @Override
65.         public void run() {
66.
     System.out.println("Running " +
     Thread.currentThread().getName());
67.
     methodExecInThread();
68.
69.         }
70.      });
71.
72.    //provide Runnable object to submit
73.    Future<?> task2Future = executorService.submit(new
     Runnable() {
74.
75.         @Override
76.         public void run() {
```

```
77.
    System.out.println("Running " +
 Thread.currentThread().getName());
78.
    methodExecInThread();
79.
80.            }
81.       });
82.
83.    /* check if both tasks have completed - if not sleep
 current thread
84.     * for 1 second and check again
85.    */
86.    //check if both the task is completed - blocking
87.    while(!task1Future.isDone() || !task2Future.isDone()){
88.                                System.out.println("Both
 the task is in progress..");
89.    //sleep for some time
90.    Thread.sleep(2000);
91.    }
92.    // tasks are done
93.    System.out.println("Both tasks are completed.");
94.    }
95.    finally{
96.    //Initiates an orderly shutdown in which previously
 submitted
97.    //tasks are executed, but no new tasks will be accepted.
98.     executorService.shutdown();
99.     }
100.    }
101.
102.
103.    public static void main(String[] args) throws
 InterruptedException {
104.    ExecutorServiceRunnableTest esObj = new
 ExecutorServiceRunnableTest();
105.
106.    System.out.println("Using execute method of
 executorService: ");
107.                   esObj.executorServiceExecuteExample();
108.    System.out.println("Using submit method of
 executorService: ");
109.    esObj.executorServiceSubmitExample();
110.
111.
112.    }
113.
114. }
```

142

Output:

```
Using execute method of executorService:
Running pool-1-thread-1
Running pool-1-thread-2
Using submit method of executorService:
Running pool-2-thread-1
Both the task is in progress..
Running pool-2-thread-2
Both the task is in progress..
Both the task is in progress..
Both tasks are completed.
```

In above example ExecutorService execute and submit method is being used with Runnable object to create thread. We are using Executors class to create ExecutorService object, Executors class provides factory method that make the life easy.

Below is the example of ExecutorService with callable interface.

```
1.  public class ExecutorServiceCallableTest {
2.
3.    Double methodExecInThread(){
4.
5.      try {
6.          Thread.sleep(5000);
7.      } catch (InterruptedException ex) {
8.          ex.printStackTrace();
9.      }
10.         return Math.random();
11.     }
12.
13.    Callable<Double> createCallable(){
14.
15.      return new Callable<Double>() {
16.
17.        public Double call() throws Exception {

18.
19.                return methodExecInThread();

20.          }

21.      };
22.    }
23.
24.    public void executorServiceSubmitExample() throws
    InterruptedException, ExecutionException{
25.
```

```
26.    ExecutorService executorService =
   Executors.newFixedThreadPool(2);
27.
28.    try{
29.
30.      Future<Double> task1Future =
   executorService.submit(new Callable<Double>() {
31.
32.      @Override
33.      public Double call() throws Exception {
34.          Double returnVal = methodExecInThread();
35.              return returnVal;
36.      }
37.    });
38.
39.    Future<Double> task2Future = executorService.submit(new
   Callable<Double>() {
40.
41.      @Override
42.      public Double call() throws Exception {
43.          Double returnVal = methodExecInThread();
44.          return returnVal;
45.      }
46.    });
47.
48.    Double value1 = task1Future.get();
49.
    System.out.println(String.format("Task1 Returned value:
   "+value1));
50.    Double value2 = task2Future.get();
51.
    System.out.println(String.format("Task2 Returned value:
   "+value2));
52.  }
53.  finally{
54.          executorService.shutdown();

55.    }
56.  }
57.
58.  public void executorServiceExecuteExample() throws
   InterruptedException, ExecutionException{
59.
60.    ExecutorService executorService =
   Executors.newFixedThreadPool(8);
61.
62.    try{
63.
```

```
64.        Collection<Callable<Double>> callables = new
    ArrayList<>();
65.
66.     // create two Callables
67.                          callables.add(createCallable());
68.                          callables.add(createCallable());
69.
70.     //invoke all Callables
71.     List<Future<Double>> returnValueList =
    executorService.invokeAll(callables);
72.
73.     for (Future<Double> future : returnValueList) {
74.       //get result when it becomes available call blocking
    method get()
75.           Double value = future.get();
76.
    System.out.println(String.format("Returned value:
    "+value));
77.           }
78.        }
79.     finally{
80.         executorService.shutdown();

81.        }
82.     }
83.
84.     public static void main(String[] args) throws
    InterruptedException, ExecutionException {
85.        ExecutorServiceCallableTest esObj = new
    ExecutorServiceCallableTest();
86.
87.     System.out.println("Using submit method of
    executorService: ");
88.     esObj.executorServiceSubmitExample();
89.
90.     System.out.println("Using execute method of
    executorService: ");
91.                 esObj.executorServiceExecuteExample();
92.     }
93.  }
```

Output:
```
Using submit method of executorService:
Task1 Returned value: 0.15740515338219585
Task2 Returned value: 0.663472678002132
Using execute method of executorService:
Returned value: 0.5916177969613918
Returned value: 0.4428742894665886
```

In above example you can see how we are using callable and taking returns as future object. Calling get() method that is the blocking method of Future wait until thread is completed and return value is available.

ScheduledExecutorService

ScheduledExecutorService derived from ExecutorService interface that provides schedule method to create task with various delay, and it returns the task object that can be used to cancel or check execution. All schedule methods accept relative delays and periods as arguments, not absolute times or dates. It is a simple matter to transform an absolute time represented as a Date to the required form. For example, to schedule at a certain future date, you can use: schedule(task, date.getTime() - System.currentTimeMillis(), TimeUnit.MILLISECONDS). below is the example.

```
1.  public class ScheduledExecutorTest {
2.
3.      public static void main(String[] args) {
4.
5.          ScheduledExecutorService executorSvc =
    Executors.newScheduledThreadPool(1);
6.
7.          Runnable taskTwo = () -> System.out.println("Running
    Task Two at - " + LocalTime.now());
8.
9.      // call immediately
10.     taskOne();
11.
12.     //schedule this task to run after 10 seconds
13.     executorSvc.schedule(taskTwo, 10, TimeUnit.SECONDS);
14.
15.     //call immediately
16.     taskThree();
17.
18.     executorSvc.shutdown();
19.
20.     }
21.
22.     public static void taskOne() {
23.         System.out.println("Running Task One at - "+
    LocalTime.now());
24.     }
25.
26.     public static void taskThree() {
```

```
27.        System.out.println("Running task Three at - "+
    LocalTime.now());
28.    }
29.
30. }
```

Output:
```
Running Task One at - 19:52:47.442831
Running task Three at - 19:52:47.445799
Running Task Two at - 19:52:57.449282
```

In above example you can see Task One and Task two ran immediately, but Task Three ran after 10 second of Task One. In above example I am using Runnable, similarly you can use callable interface.

Thread Pools

You already saw in above example I have used thread pools. In most of the example I have used FixedThreadPool which consists of worker threads.

The fixed thread pool is very common in which you always specified number of threads running. You can see in above examples how fixed thread pool is getting created. The thread pool has its internal queue, whenever you submit any task, it places that task in internal pool. You can use factory method of class Executors, that provides factory methods to create all different kind of executors.

Fork/Join Framework

Fork/Join framework was introduced in Java 7. Fork/Join is an implementation of ExecutorService interface that helps you to take advantage of multiple processors. Fork splits the tasks into several subtasks that can be executed concurrently, and join is the process that keeps waiting for the completion of all the subtask created by fork and joins the results from all subtasks. Fork/Join framework is ideal for recursive methods. There are no guarantees that fork/join framework will distribute the work evenly between the threads. ForkJoinPool is a thread pool that manage the execution of ForkJoinTask. ForJoinTask is an abstract class that defines the tasks that runs in ForkJoinPool. ForkJoinTask provides fork(), join(), and invoke(), invokeAll() methods.

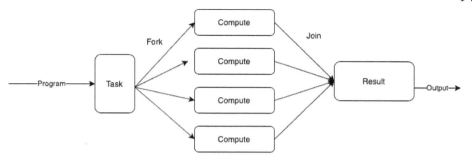

ForkJoinTask has two subclass, RecursiveAction class that can be used for tasks that does not return anything (void tasks), and RecursiveTask<> class that can be used for tasks that can return something. Both class overrides the compute() method from base class ForkJoinTask, in compute() method you need to write the tasks logic.

Starting java 8, Stream API use fork/join framework internally when you do parallel stream. Also when you call parallelSort() method of java.util.Arrays class, it sorts the array by using fork/join framework internally.

Concurrent Collections

Concurrent collections are grouped into java.util.concurrent package that is separate from java collection API. Concurrent collections are collections API that is specially designed, developed, and optimized for synchronized multithreaded access. Concurrent collections can be easily categorized along with the collection APIs. Below are the concurrent collections.

BlockingQueue

BlockingQueue interface is extended from Collection, Iterable, and Queue interface. The classes ArrayBlockingQueue, DelayQueue, LinkedBlockingDeque, LinkedBlockingQueue, LinkedTransferQueue, PriorityBlockingQueue, and SynchronousQueue are the implementation of BlockingQueue interface. I have already explained the queue example in collections chapter.

BlockingQueue implementations are thread safe. All queuing methods achieve their effects atomically using internal locks or other forms of concurrency control. BlockingQueue defines a first-in-first-out data structure that blocks or times out when you attempt to add to a full queue or retrieve from an empty queue.

ConcurrentMap

ConcurrentMap interface extends the Map interface and provides the same functionality as Map. ConcurrentMap is a thread safe Map that provides atomicity. As with other concurrent collections, actions in a thread prior to placing an object into a ConcurrentMap as a key or value happen-before actions subsequent to the access or removal of that object from the ConcurrentMap in another thread.

Happens-Before is defined as the results of a write by one thread are guaranteed to be visible to a read by another thread only if the write operation happens-before the read operation. The synchronized and volatile constructs, as well as the Thread.start() and Thread.join() methods, can form happens-before relationships.

ConcurrentHashMap

ConcurrentHashMap class is the implementation of ConcurrentMap interface. ConcurrentHashMap is similar to the HashMap that can be used in multithreaded environment because of its thread-safe properties. But unlike HashMap, ConcurrentHashMap does not allow null as key or value.

ConcurrentSkipListMap

ConcurrentSkipListMap is similar to the TreeMap. The map is sorted according to the natural ordering of its keys, or by a Comparator provided at map creation time, depending on which constructor is used. Because of asynchronous behavior of ConcurrentSkipListMap determining the size is not state forward, it requires traversal of the Map, and during traversal some thread might be modifying some element, so finding size is not a constant time operation in ConcurrentSkipListMap. ConcurrentSkipListMap does not allow null as key or value.

Atomic Variables

For atomic operation on single variable, java.util.concurrent.atomic package defines classes, that can be used in multithreading environment. It provides thread safe programming on single variable.

The atomic method compareAndSet(int expected, int update) automatically sets the value to the given updated value. Here expected argument is for expected value and update argument is for new value. Upon success it returns true, and if actual value is not equal to expected value, this method returns false.

Instances of classes AtomicBoolean, AtomicInteger, AtomicLong, and AtomicReference each provide access and updates to a single variable of the corresponding type. Each class also provides appropriate utility methods for that type.

Below is one example of using AtomicInteger class.

```
1.  class AtomicTest {
2.      private AtomicInteger atomInt = new AtomicInteger(0);
3.
4.      public void increment() {
5.          atomInt.incrementAndGet();
6.      }
7.
8.      public void decrement() {
9.          atomInt.decrementAndGet();
10.      }
11.
12.     public int value() {
13.         return atomInt.get();
14.      }
15. }
```

7 Java 8 features

Java 8, that was released in 2014, is not new for java developers now. Most of you might already using it. Java 8 was a major release of java; it was a big release after java 5. Java 8 came with lots of feature and enhancements, the main features are listed as below.

- Lambda Expression.
- Stream API.
- Method References.
- Default and static method for interfaces.
- New Date and Time API.
- Optional.
- CompletableFuture.

We will discuss on each feature here. I am considering that you have basic idea about java 8 features.

Lambda Expression

Lambda Expression is the biggest feature release of java 8. Java introduced functional programming with this feature. To use lambda expression, you must have functional interface. The functional interface you can create, or you can use any of the existing functional interface.

Functional Interface

A functional interface is an interface that can have one and only one abstract method. Functional interface must have one abstract method. Now let's say you have created any interface with one abstract method, and you can call it functional interface, yes correct.

Lambda expression can be used only with the functional interface. For example, Runnable is a functional interface because this interface has only one abstract method run().

Now you have created a functional interface with one abstract method to use it in lambda expression and someone added one more abstract method in that interface. To restrict that you can use @functionalInterface annotation for functional interface, this annotation is not mandatory but benefit of using this annotation is if someone will add more abstract method in functional interface or someone delete the abstract method from functional interface then it will give compile time error. It is a good practice to use @functionalInterface annotation if you are creating functional interface. Below id the functional interface as it has only one abstract method.

```
1. @FunctionalInterface
2. public interface TestFuncInterface {
3.
4.   void test();
5.
6. }
```

Functional interface may have multiple default methods, as below.

```
1. @FunctionalInterface
```

```
2. public interface TestFuncInterface {
3.
4.   void test();
5.
6.   default void defaultMethod1() {
7.
8.   }
9.
10.          default void defaultMethod2() {
11.
12.             }
13.
14.  }
```

Above interface is also a functional interface as it has only one abstract method test().

Lambda Expression Basics

Lambda expression is same as the anonymous function, lambda provides a simpler way to represent anonymous function. If your concepts of anonymous functions are not clear, please take a look into anonymous functions in detail. Lambda expression is anonymous function that does not have the name. Lambda expression can be used for functional interface, that has only one abstract method. You do not have to mention function name as it will always use the only abstract method you have defined in functional interface. You already know name of method, argument types, and return type.

Java provides comparator interface that is a functional interface. Now see below example how you can use comparator interface using anonymous method without lambda expression.

```
1. public class Dancers {
2.
3.   String name;
4.   Integer age;
5.
6.   public Dancers(String name, Integer age) {
7.          super();
8.          this.name = name;
9.          this.age = age;
10.         }
11.
12.         public String getName() {
13.            return name;
14.         }
15.         public void setName(String name) {
```

```java
16.                    this.name = name;
17.            }
18.            public Integer getAge() {
19.                    return age;
20.            }
21.            public void setAge(Integer age) {
22.                    this.age = age;
23.            }
24.
25.      public static void main(String[] args) {
26.
27.          Comparator<Dancers> dancerComparatorByAge = new
    Comparator<>() {
28.              public int compare(Dancers a1, Dancers a2){
29.                  return a1.getAge().compareTo(a2.getAge());
30.              }
31.            };
32.
33.          Dancers d1 = new Dancers("D1", 22);
34.          Dancers d2 = new Dancers("D2", 19);
35.          Dancers d3 = new Dancers("D3", 25);
36.
37.          List<Dancers> dancersList = new ArrayList<>();
38.          dancersList.add(d1);
39.          dancersList.add(d2);
40.          dancersList.add(d3);
41.
42.          System.out.println("Dancers before sorting: ");
43.          for(Dancers d : dancersList) {
44.                          System.out.println(d.getName());
45.          }
46.
47.          Collections.sort(dancersList, dancerComparatorByAge);
48.
49.          System.out.println("Dancers after sorting: ");
50.          for(Dancers d : dancersList) {
51.                          System.out.println(d.getName());
52.          }
53.
54.      }
55.
56.  }
```

Output:
```
Dancers before sorting:
D1
D2
D3
```

```
Dancers after sorting:
D2
D1
D3
```

In above program you can see anonymous function

```
1.  Comparator<Dancers> dancerComparatorByAge = new
    Comparator<>() {
2.     public int compare(Dancers a1, Dancers a2){
3.        return a1.getAge().compareTo(a2.getAge());
4.           }
5.     };
```

I am creating comparator using above anonymous method and passing it to the second argument of sort method.

```
Collections.sort(dancersList, dancerComparatorByAge);
```

Here sort method's first argument is collection type that is list and second argument is of comparator type. Because Comparator is functional interface, instead of anonymous method above you can use lambda expression as below.

```
Comparator<Dancers> dancerComparatorByAge = (x,y)->{return
x.getAge().compareTo(y.getAge());};
```

In above lambda expression example, you already knows that you are using comparator that has only one method compare(). Above (x, y) -> implies that compare method that is taking two object x and y of type Dancers, because you are casting comparator in Dancers object. And after arrow -> is the implementation of compare method with two Dancers object x and y. Here in method of lambda expression (x,y)-> {...} class name is optional you can write the class name with object x and y like (Dancers x, Dancers y) -> {...}. Below is the equivalent lambda expression.

```
Comparator<Dancers> dancerComparatorByAge = (Dancers x, Dancers
y)->{return x.getAge().compareTo(y.getAge());};
```

The syntax of lambda expression is (parameters)->expression or (parameters)->{ statements}.

Stream API

Stream is a sequence of elements that can be processed with operations. Stream is not a data structure like array or collection, it is a way to process data can be flow through the stream. Process data means you can do some operation on data easily and effectively without writing much code. Stream supports both sequential and parallel operation over dataset. Always keep in mind that stream has no storage. Stream represent the data that is stored in some data structure.

Stream can be represented as sequence of infinite element. Stream API consists of java.util.stream classes that supports functional-style operations on streams of elements, like map-reduce transformations on collections. Here is the example.

```
1. // List of String
2. List<String> strings = Arrays.asList("abc", "bcd", "cde");
3. //sequential Stream over the list elements
4. Stream<String> seqStream = strings.stream();
5. //parallel Stream over the list elements
6. Stream<String> parallelStream  = strings.parallelStream();
```

Stream method create sequential stream over collections like list in above example, similarly parallelStream method creates parallel stream that may execute operation in multiple threads. ParallelStream use fork/join framework to break operations into multiple threads and joins to get the result that utilizes maximum of multiple processors.

Stream operations and pipeline

Stream pipeline consists of a source, intermediate, and terminal operation. A source can be any collection, an array, a generator function, or an I/O channel. Intermediate operation can be Stream.filter() or Stream.map(). There can be multiple intermediate operation in one stream pipeline. A stream pipeline can consist of only source and terminal operation, intermediate operations are optional. There must be a source and the stream pipeline must be ended with terminal operation. Example of terminal operation is Stream.forEach(), Stream.reduce(), Stream.sum(), Stream.count(), etc. Intermediate operations also called as non-terminal operations.

Stream does not store any data; it always works on collection or source data who stores the actual data and produced result by terminal operation can be stored again in collection or can be printed.

You can obtain stream first to work on it, the first thing you can do is use the stream() method to obtain stream from source. Like Stream<String> stream = listOfString.stream(); There are two method to get the stream, stream() and parallelStream(). The stream() method returns sequential stream whereas parallelStream() returns a parallel stream that divides the tasks into multiple threads (fork) and joins to get the result.

Intermediate operations are further divided into stateless and stateful operations. Stateless operations, such as filter and map, retain no state from previously seen element when processing a new element -- each element can be processed independently of operations on other elements. Stateful operations, such as distinct and sorted, may incorporate state from previously seen elements when processing new elements.

Stream API Examples

Here are few examples that may help you understand the stream API.

```java
1.  public class Test {
2.
3.    public static void main(String[] args) {
4.
5.    //List of Person
6.    List<Person> persons = new ArrayList<>();
7.    Person p1 = new Person(25);
8.    Person p2 = new Person(31);
9.    Person p3 = new Person(17);
10.   persons.add(p1);
11.   persons.add(p2);
12.   persons.add(p3);
13.
14.   // List of Integers
15.   List<Integer> intList = Arrays.asList(1,2,3,4,5);

16.
17.   //Sum of all the element of list
18.   Integer sum = intList.stream().reduce(0, Integer::sum);

19.
20.   //Sum of all the element of list
21.   Integer sum1 = intList.stream().mapToInt(a->a).sum();

22.
23.   //skip first two element and take next five element
```

```
24.  List<Integer> sublist =
     intList.stream().skip(2).limit(5).collect(Collectors.toList
     ());
25.
26.  /// distinct element of a list
27.  List<Integer> distinctList =
     intList.stream().distinct().collect(Collectors.toList());
28.
29.  //Sort the list
30.  List<Integer> sortedList =
     intList.stream().sorted().collect(Collectors.toList());
31.
32.  //Print the list in reverse order
33.
     intList.stream().collect(Collectors.toCollection(LinkedList
     ::new)).descendingIterator().forEachRemaining(System.out::p
     rintln);
34.
35.  ///print all Person whose age is more than 20, also peek
     the element
36.  persons.stream().map(p-
     >p.getAge()).peek(System.out::println).filter(age-
     >age>20).forEach(System.out::println);
37.
38.  ///count of the person whose age is more than 20
39.  long l = persons.stream().filter(x-
     >x.getAge()>20).count();
40.
41.  //find the first person whose age is more than 20 or
     return null
42.  persons.stream().map(x->x.getAge()).filter(age-
     >age>20).findFirst().orElse(null);
43.
44.  String s = "1 2 3 4 5 6 7 8 9 10";
45.
46.  ///convert string s to list of integer by splitting with
     space
47.  List<Integer> ints =
     Arrays.stream(s.split("\\s+")).map(Integer::parseInt).colle
     ct(Collectors.toList());
48.  // each integer of list to the power of 2.0
49.  List<Double> pow2 = ints.stream().map(x -> Math.pow(2.0,
     x)).collect(Collectors.toList());
50.
51.  ///convert to the list of string in specific format
52.  List<String> doubled = ints.stream().map(k -> k + "_" +
     k).collect(Collectors.toList());
53.
54.  /// Split the words to make list of String of words
```

```java
55.   List<String> words = Arrays.stream("Hello how are you
      doing".split("\\s+")).collect(Collectors.toList());
56.
57.   //join the words again to make complete string without
      seperator
58.   String noDelimiter =
      words.stream().collect(Collectors.joining());
59.
60.   //join the words again to make complete string with comma
      seperator
61.   String withDelimiter = words.stream().map(it ->
      Integer.toString(it.length())).collect(Collectors.joining("
      , "));
62.
63.   //Create a map of Words as key and length of word as value
64.   Map<String, Integer> map =
      words.stream().collect(Collectors.toMap(Function.identity()
      , String::length));
65.
66.   //Create map with word length as key and words as value
67.   Map<Integer, List<String>> wordsByLength =
      words.stream().collect(Collectors.groupingBy(String::length
      ));
68.
69.      }
70.
71.   }
72.
73.   class Person{
74.      Integer age;
75.
76.      public Integer getAge() {
77.           return age;
78.      }
79.
80.      public void setAge(Integer age) {
81.           this.age = age;
82.      }
83.
84.      public Person(Integer age) {
85.           super();
86.           this.age = age;
87.      }
88.   }
```

Method References

Method References are the shorthand of lambda expression. You can use method reference for any lambda expression for existing method. Lambda expression gets used in place of anonymous method. Whenever you use lambda expression to just call an existing method, you can use method reference in that situation. Method reference is cleaner approach that is easy to read. It can be used just for calling of existing method by name in place of lambda expression.

If you are using lambda expression as below –

```
something -> System.out.println(something)
```

Above code can be written in cleaner way using method reference as –
```
System.out::println
```

Now see this example closely

```
1. // List of Integers
2. List<Integer> intList = Arrays.asList(1,2,2,3,4,5);
3.
4. //Convert List to Set and print unique value
5. intList.stream().collect(Collectors.toSet()).forEach(value-
   >System.out.print(value));
```

Output:
```
12345
```

Now the same code can be written with method reference as below.

```
1. // List of Integers
2. List<Integer> intList = Arrays.asList(1,2,2,3,4,5);
3.
4. //Convert List to Set and print unique value
5. intList.stream().collect(Collectors.toSet()).forEach(System
   .out::print);
```

In above code System.out::print will do the same job as `value->System.out.print(value)` and output will be same as above. Now let's see another Example.

```
1. // List of Integers
2. List<Integer> intList = Arrays.asList(1,2,2,3,4,5);
3. //Sum of all the element of list
4. Integer sum = intList.stream().reduce(0,(a,b)->
   Integer.sum(a, b));
5. System.out.println(sum);
```

Output:

17

In above code lambda expression `(a,b)->Integer.sum(a, b)` is being used to calculate sum in reduce. Using method reference you can just write it as `Integer::sum` and it will do the same job as below.

```
1. // List of Integers
2. List<Integer> intList = Arrays.asList(1,2,2,3,4,5);
3. //Sum of all the element of list
4. Integer sum = intList.stream().reduce(0, Integer::sum);
5. System.out.println(sum);
```

You can see in above code reduce operation is easy to read compare to the lambda version of method.

Always remember, that method reference can be used only in place of lambda expression, where lambda expression is being used to call the existing method. If lambda expression is being used to implement any method, you cannot replace that with method reference.

Default and static method for interfaces.

Starting java 8, interface gets two types of methods, default and static method. This enhancement of interface, interface become more capable than ever. Let's examine each of these two methods.

Default method

Default method is a method in interface that you can have with body. You can define a method with default keyword with body, and any class that will implements this interface, default method will be available in that class.

Now first question may come in your mind is, if you can have method with body in interface as well as you can have abstract method in interface, then what is the difference between interface and abstract class now? Yes, it became almost similar, now the difference is that, you can have constructor in abstract class, that you cannot have in interface.

Now you can have method with definition in interface, it is almost similar to the abstract class, and you can implement as many interfaces as you want in a class. This way you can use multiple inheritance now because of introduction of default method in interface. What about diamond problem? You will not get diamond problem as they specially designed default method and set the rules to avoid diamond problem.

Diamond problem is a problem of multiple inheritance when the class will get two version of method, see in below diagram.

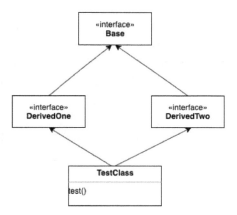

As in above diagram Base interface has default method test(), DerivedOne and DerivedTwo interface gets a copy of test() method. Now TestClass will get two version of test() method, one through DerivedOne interface and one through DerivedTwo interface. That will create ambiguity for TestClass, TestClass don't know which version of test() method to use. In this situation, TestClass has to override its own version of test() method, that TestClass implementation of test() method will get called and diamond problem will not occur. If TestClass will not override test() method, it will show you error, even though test() is default method defined in Base interface, to resolve diamond problem in java 8 , it made compulsory to override. Default method in interface can be private as well in java 8.

Default methods in interface allow developers to add new methods to the interface without affecting the classes that implements these interfaces. Default method in java 8 is introduced to add new methods to the existing interfaces, in such way they are backward compatible. Below is the example of default method.

```
1. public interface EnhancedInterface {
2.
3.    default void additionalMethod() {
4.            System.out.println("I am default method");
5.    }
6. }
```

Static Method

Starting java 8, you can have static method with complete definition in interface. It is like the default method that you do not have to implement in the implementation class. You cannot override static method by rule as well, that is the main difference between default and static method in interface, default method can be overridden in derived interface or class. Like default method you can add static method to the existing interface safely without affecting the implementation classes. Static method in interface can be private in Java 8.

Usually you create utility method as static method in class. Now with this new feature you can have all the utility method at one place in interface instead of defining them in class. Below is the example of static method.

```
1. public interface EnhancedInterface {
2.
3.    static void utilityMethod() {
4.            System.out.println("Hello from static method");
5.    }
6. }
```

New Date and Time API

Java 8 introduced new date and time API to overcome the drawbacks of java.util.Date and java.util.Calendar. The new date and time API is in java.time package that provides API for dates, times, instants, and durations. The earlier Date and Calendar were not thread safe and it was developer's responsibility to make them thread safe.

The new Date and Time API is thread safe. All the core classes of new Date and Time API are immutable and represent well-defined values. The following main classes are available for new Date and Time API.

Instant: A numerical timestamp that represents instantaneous point on the timeline. It can be used to record event timestamp in the application. *Instant* class is mutable and thread safe. It can store result from System.currentTimeMillis(). You can use abstract class Clock to get instance like:

```
1.  Instant instant =
    Clock.system(ZoneId.systemDefault()).instant();
2.  System.out.println(instant);
```

Output:
```
2020-08-04T23:06:01.128041Z
```

LocalDate: LocalDate is an immutable and thread-safe class that stores a date without a time, it can be used to store a date like birthday. Below is the example.

```
1.  LocalDate date = LocalDate.now();
2.  System.out.println(date);
```

Output:
```
2020-08-04
```

LocalTime: LocalTime is an immutable and thread-safe class that stores a time without date, it can be used to store shop's open and close time. Below is the example.

```
1.  LocalTime time = LocalTime.now();
2.  System.out.println(time);
```

Output:
```
19:29:11.029231
```

LocalDateTime: LocalDateTime is an immutable and thread-safe class that can be used to store date and time together. Below is the example.

```
1.  LocalDateTime ldt = LocalDateTime.now();
2.  System.out.println(ldt);
```

Output:
```
2020-08-04T19:54:27.853509
```

ZonedDateTime: ZonedDateTime is an immutable and thread-safe class that stores date and time with time zone. Below is the example.

```
1. ZonedDateTime zdt = ZonedDateTime.now();
2. System.out.println(zdt);
```

Output:
```
2020-08-04T19:59:00.972997-04:00[America/New_York]
```

Duration: A Duration is an immutable and thread-safe class that stores quantity or amount of time in terms of seconds and nanoseconds. You can get the duration in hour, minutes, days, based on your use case. You can get difference between two time and get duration. Below is the example.

```
1. Duration duration = Duration.ofMinutes(30);
2. System.out.println(duration); // Output: PT30M
3. System.out.println(duration.toSeconds()); //Output:1800
4. LocalDateTime dateTimeInJuly = LocalDateTime.of(2020,
   Month.JULY, 30, 12, 00, 00);
5. LocalDateTime dateTimeInAug = LocalDateTime.of(2020,
   Month.AUGUST, 4, 12, 00, 00);
6. Duration diff = Duration.between(dateTimeInJuly,
   dateTimeInAug);
7. System.out.println(diff); // Output: PT120H
8. System.out.println(diff.toHours()); // Output: 120
9. System.out.println(diff.toMinutes()); // Output: 7200
```

Period: Period is an immutable and thread-safe class that stores quantity or amount of time in terms of Years, Months, and Days. Time based equivalent class of Period is Duration, that store amount of time in Hours, minutes, seconds, and nanoseconds. Below is the example.

```
1. //Period of 30 Days
2. Period p1 = Period.ofDays(30);
3. System.out.println(p1); //Output: P30D
4. LocalDate t1 = LocalDate.of(2019, Month.JULY, 30);
5. LocalDate t2 = LocalDate.of(2020, Month.AUGUST, 4);
6. Period p2 = Period.between(t1, t2);
7. System.out.println(p2); //Output: P1Y5D
```

Optional

Java 8 introduced new class Optional<T>. Optional is like a single value container that either contains a value or empty. You can avoid NullPointerException by using Optional. Optional method forces you to explicitly check presence or absence of a value. If value is present isPresent() will return true and get() will return the value(). There are other methods that depends on presence or absence of a contained value are provided, like orElse() returns a default value if value is not present and ifPresent() executes a block of code if value is present. Below is an example.

```
1. public class OptionalTest {
2.
3.    public static void main(String[] args) {
4.
5.    Computer comp1 = checkComputer(new Computer("10.20.1.135",
   "ABCD1235"));
6.    System.out.println(comp1.hostName);
7.
8.    Computer comp2 = checkComputer(null);
9.    System.out.println(comp2.hostName);
10.
11.   }
12.
13.   public static Computer checkComputer(Computer obj){
14.
15.   return Optional.ofNullable(obj).orElse(new
   Computer("NoIP", "NoHost"));
16.
17.   }
18.   }
19.
20.   class Computer{
21.   String ip;
22.   String hostName;
23.   public Computer(String ip, String hostName) {
24.           super();
25.           this.ip = ip;
26.           this.hostName = hostName;
27.   }
28.
29.   }
```

Output:

In above example checkComputer() method returns the default value in case Computer object is null, it will save you from NullPointerException. Optional extensively get used in stream APIs in which lots of methods returns the Optional to save NullPointerException. Stream interface method findAny(), findFirst(), max(), min(), reduce(), etc. is returning the Optional<T>. There are three primitive Optional are available in java 8, that is OptionalDouble, OptionalInt, and OptionalLong.

CompletableFuture

Future was introduced in java 5 to get result of the asynchronous computation. You have already seen the use of future in Callable interface. CompletableFuture is introduced in java 8 that can combine the steps from one asynchronous method with other steps from different asynchronous methods. CompletableFuture implements CompletionStage interface that defines the contract for asynchronous computation steps combined with the other steps.

As CompletableFuture implemented Future interface as well, you can use CompletableFuture in all places where you can use Future interface. CompletableFuture implements two interfaces, one is Future, and another is CompletionStage interface.

Below is the simple example of CompletableFuture.

```
1. CompletableFuture<String> cf
2.     = CompletableFuture.supplyAsync(() -> "Hello");
3.
4. CompletableFuture<String> cf1 = cf
5.     .thenApply(s -> s + " World");
6.
7. String finalResult = cf1.get();
8. System.out.println(finalResult);
```

Output:
Hello World

8   Unit Testing

Unit Testing is a testing method by which you can test individual unit of source code. A unit is smallest possible of source code segment that can be tested independently. For each possible unit of code should have test cases that checks if code is correct and working as expected.

To write unit test in java you can use Junit test suite. The latest Junit suite version is Junit 5.0. Junit 5 supports java 8 or higher only. In this chapter we will use Junit 5 to write any test.

Junit Tests

To write a test case you can create a separate class with the same name of your actual class and end the class name with Tests. You should write test case in separate folder structure. Your test cases should go to the separate test directory. Below is the example of one simple test case.

```
1.  class HelloFeatureTest {
2.
3.    @Test
4.    void test() {
5.            assertTrue(true);
6.    }
7.
8. }
```

Above test class *HelloFeatureTest* is created for the class *HelloFeature*. Here @Test annotation of Junit meaning a unit test. Every unit test method should have @Test annotation. There is other annotation we will discuss below.

Parameterized test

Parameterized test can be used to run a test multiple time with different arguments. This can be declared with annotation @ParameterizedTest very similar to the @Test annotation. In below example @ValueSource is being used to pass different arguments.

```
1.  class HelloFeatureTest {
2.
3.    HelloFeature obj = new HelloFeature();
4.
5.    @ParameterizedTest
6.    @ValueSource(ints= {2,4,8,56})
7.    void isEvenTest(Integer i) {
8.            assertTrue(obj.isEven(i));
9.        }
10. }
```

In above example code I am running parameterized test. @ValueSource annotation is being used to pass multiple arguments. In @ValueSource ints={} is integer array. Similarly you can pass String array as an argument with strings={}. Above test case will run four times for four different integer arguments, that means above test is equivalent to the four @Test with four different arguments.

The @ValueSource annotation supports short, byte, int, long, float, double, char, boolean, string, and class arguments.

Repeated test

Repeated test is used to repeat the same test to the given number of times. Below is the example.

```
1.    @RepeatedTest(5)
2.    void isEnenTest1() {
3.            assertTrue(true);
4.    }
```

Above test will execute 5 times.

Dynamic test

Dynamic tests can be created by using @TestFactory annotation. The @TestFactory must returns a single DynamicNode or a Stream, Collection, Iterable, Iterator, or an array of DynamicNode instances. A DynamicTest is a test that is generated at runtime. DynamicTest is composed of a display name and executable. Executable is a @FunctionalInterface, that means you can provide lambda expressions or functional references in the DynamicTest implementation. Below is the example of Dynamic Test.

```
1. HelloFeature obj = new HelloFeature();
2.
3. @TestFactory
4. Collection<DynamicTest> CollectiondynamicTests() {
5.   return Arrays.asList(
6.     DynamicTest.dynamicTest("1st dynamic test", () ->
   assertTrue(true)),
7.     DynamicTest.dynamicTest("2nd dynamic test", () ->
   assertTrue(obj.isEven(4)))
8.             );
9. }
```

The @TestFactory is different than the @Test as @BeforeEach and @AfterEach methods are not executed for Dynamic Test, but executed for @Test.

Test Method Execution Order

The @TestMethodOrder annotation can be used to control the order of execution of @Test methods. The @TestMethodOrder can be used in following way.

```
1.  @TestMethodOrder(Alphanumeric.class)
2.  class TestMethodOrderingTest {
3.
4.      @Test
5.      void Btest1() {
6.              //some test
7.      }
8.
9.      @Test
10.     void Atest1() {
11.             //some test
12.     }
13.  }
```

In above example @Test method will get executed in alphanumerical order. ATest1() gets executed before BTest1().

```
1.  @TestMethodOrder(Random.class)
2.  class TestMethodOrderingTest {
3.
4.      @Test
5.      void Btest1() {
6.              //some test
7.      }
8.
9.      @Test
10.     void Atest1() {
11.             //some test
12.     }
13.  }
```

In above example the @Test method can be executed in any random order.

```
1.  @TestMethodOrder(OrderAnnotation.class)
2.  class TestMethodOrderingTest {
3.
4.      @Test
5.      @Order(1)
6.      void testMethod1() {
```

```
7.              //some test
8.     }
9.
10.    @Test
11.    @Order(2)
12.    void testMethod2() {
13.             //some test
14.    }
15.    }
```

In above example @Test method will get executed based on the @Order annotation of test method.

Before and After @Test

The @BeforeEach method gets executed before each @Test, @TestFactory, @RepeatedTest, and @ParameterizedTest method. The @AfterEach method gets executed after each @Test, @TestFactory, @RepeatedTest, and @ParameterizedTest Method. The @BeforeAll method gets executed before all the @Test, @TestFactory, @RepeatedTest, and @ParameterizedTest method of that class. The @AfterAll method gets executed after all the @Test, @TestFactory, @RepeatedTest, and @ParameterizedTest method of that class. Below is the example.

```
1. class BeforenAfterTest {
2.
3.    @BeforeEach
4.    void setup() {
5.             // executed before each test
6.    }
7.
8.    @BeforeAll
9.    void initialize() {
10.            // Execute once before any test
11.    }
12.
13.    @Test
14.    void test1() {
15.            // some test
16.    }
17.
18.    @Test
19.    void test2() {
20.            //Some test
21.    }
```

```
22.
23.    @TestFactory
24.    Collection<DynamicTest> CollectiondynamicTests() {
25.    return Arrays.asList(
26.    DynamicTest.dynamicTest("dynamic test", () ->
     assertTrue(true))
27.             );
28.    }
29.
30.    @RepeatedTest(5)
31.    void isEnenTest1() {
32.            assertTrue(true);
33.    }
34.
35.    @ParameterizedTest
36.    @ValueSource(strings= {"hi","hello"})
37.    void isEvenTest(String s) {
38.            assertTrue(s.length()>0);
39.    }
40.
41.    @AfterEach
42.    void reinitialize() {
43.            // Execute after each test
44.    }
45.
46.    @AfterAll
47.    void cleanUp() {
48.            // Execute after all tests
49.    }
50.
51.    }
```

Mockito

Mockito is a widely used open source mocking framework that work well with Junit framework to write unit test for java. Other mocking frameworks available are EasyMock, JMock, and PowerMock.

Why Mockito

The main purpose of writing unit test is if code gets broken then unit test case should fail. If your unit test case starts failing because some other service is down, then it will defeat the purpose of unit test case. Your unit test case should not fail because the external resource like, external service or database server is not available, but your code is perfect.

To overcome the situation when external resource is not available, you should mock the call of external resources using some mocking framework. You can mock the service calls or database calls. To mock the database most of the time we use in memory database so that unit test can verify the query and transaction and do not rely on network and you can mock database connection.

Mockito API

Mockito provides APIs to make it easy to write and integrate unit test cases with Junit. Below are the details of API.

@Mock

You can use @Mock annotation to create mock object. Mockito provides mock() method to mock objects. A mock object simulates the behavior of real object and you can control the call with mock object to mock some dependency of that object by mocking with the dummy result. Below is the example to mock the object.

```
1.  @Mock
2.  SomeService someService;
```

You can mock using mock method.

```
SomeService someService = Mockito.mock(SomeService.class);
```

@InjectMocks

By using this annotation Mockito will try to inject the mock by constructor, setter, or property injection. Suppose you have created test class for ServiceManager class named ServiceManagerTest. You can use mock objects and inject mock for ServiceManager class.

```
1.  @InjectMocks
2.  ServiceManager serviceManager;
```

@Spy

Spy allow the shorthand wrapping of field instance in spy object. See the below example.

```
1.  @Spy
2.  public List<String> spyList = new ArrayList<>();
3.
4.  @Test
5.  public void spyTest() {
6.    spyList.add("hello");
7.    spyList.add("Spy");
8.
9.    Mockito.verify(spyList).add("hello");
10.   Mockito.verify(spyList).add("Spy");
11.
12.   assertEquals(2, spyList.size());
13.
14.   //Mocking Size
      Mockito.doReturn(100).when(spyList).size();
15.
16.   assertEquals(100, spyList.size()); // pass
17. }
```

In above example you can see the use of spy as well as how you can mock the return value using doReturn and when. Similarly you can mock to throw an exception like – Mockito.doThrow(ex).when(x), or you can call real method instead of dummy using Mockito.doCallRealMethod().when(x).

Code Coverage

Code coverage is also called test coverage is a measurement that measures the percentage of code gets executed through the test cases. You can have multiple test cases for same method to cover the different if/else or switch cases. There are lot of tools available to measure code coverage. One of the tools is JACOCO. You just need to add JACOCO dependency and configure JACOCO plugin in maven file. You do not need to write any code to add JACOCO code coverage tool, just adding it to maven is enough. It will generate the report after running the all unit test cases from root test folder. JACOCO report will show you that what percentage of code coverage you have achieved and what are those code segments that is still not covered with the test cases.

You can configure the reports and also you can exclude some file or exclude some package that you are not writing unit test cases. JACOCO will not consider excluded file or package to generate coverage report and in calculation of code coverage percentage.

You can find similar other tools for code coverage as well. Your organization will decide what percentage of code coverage is compulsory to pass unit test cases in CI/CD pipeline.

TDD

Test Driven Development (TDD) is a software development technique where you write unit test case first and then write or improve code to pass the test cases. Software developed using TDD is proven to meet requirements. Following set of rule defines the TDD.

1. Write a unit test case that describe an aspect of your program.
2. Run the test, this test will fail or error out because you are yet to write the program you have written test for.
3. Write the simplest possible code to pass the test.
4. Write another test for possible aspect of the same program.
5. Refactor the code with just enough change to pass the test.
6. Keep repeating the steps from 3 to 5 until your method is complete with its functionality.

Below are the benefits of TDD.

1. Reduce the defect rate.
2. Easy to make change in code, or easy and less error prone maintenance.
3. Improve design quality of code.

However above benefits come with the cost of increase of development effort. The increased development efforts get compensated with less maintenance effort and improved code quality.

9   Miscellaneous concepts

This chapter will cover all the concepts that is not covered in book and is needed to succeed in interview.

Reflection

Reflection in java is used to examine or modify the runtime behavior of methods, class, and interface at runtime. Classes for reflection in defined in the java.lang.reflect package. Reflection can be used to inspect and dynamically call class, method, and properties at run time. You can call getclass() to get the class name. You can call getclass(). getPackage(); to get package information at runtime. Similary you can call getMethod() , getDeclaredFields().

```
Method[] methods = Test.class.getMethods();
```

The above line will fetch all the methods.

```
1.  for(Method method : methods){
2.      System.out.println("method Name = " +
    method.getName());
3.  }
```

The above code will print the method names.

Reflection breaks the abstraction and encapsulation by accessing private methods and variable. You can access private method and variable using reflection by using getMethod() and invoke() methods.

But you will be able to access the method or variable if you already know the name. In case of method, you must know the method name and its parameter to invoke it.

Accessing method and variable using reflection is a performance hit on your code and it should be avoided in the code. Calling same method through reflection will have big performance overhead than calling the same method without reflection.

Java 9 Features

Java 9 came with some important features that we will discuss here. The most important feature java 9 introduced was modularity in java language called jigsaw project.

Jigsaw project

The world is changing now, and we are moving away from monolithic system. Java also feels that it is becoming a big monolithic system by using big monolithic jar to develop java-based application. The advantage of this change is JVM will start lightweight and will consume less memory. Jars are divided based on modules and only those modules will be loaded which it requires. It provides modular JDK and Modular run time image. You can define module using module keyword. You can use require keyword in module to indicate on which module it is dependent on.

Java 9 introduced new file format named .jmod that allow including native code, configuration files, and other data that do not fit into jar files. It also provides jlink tool to assemble and optimize a set of modules and their dependencies into a custom runtime image.

Java 9 also introduces a command line tool for java dependency analysis called **Jdeps**. It analyzes statically declared dependency between classes and result can be aggregated to package or jar level.

Factory method for collection

Java 9 introduced new factory methods for collections that will help to create collection object inline. Below id the example of new factory method of(). Give attention to the blank Collections (List, Set, or Map) created using factory method. Here once you even created blank collection using of factory method, you cannot modify the collection by adding any element.

```
1.  List<Integer> intList = List.of(1,2,3,4,5);
2.
3.  System.out.println(intList);
4.
5.  Set<String> wordSet = Set.of("Apple", "Bag", "Cat", "Dog");
    // cannot be modified
6.
7.  System.out.println(wordSet);
8.
9.  Map<Integer, String> testMap = Map.of(1,"A", 2, "B", 3 ,
    "C");// cannot be modified
10.
11.  System.out.println(testMap);
12.
13.  List<Integer> emptyList = List.of(); //cannot modify, not
    of any use
14.
15.  System.out.println(emptyList);
16.
17.  Map<Integer, String> emptyMap = Map.of();
18.
19.  System.out.println(emptyMap);
```

Output:
```
[1, 2, 3, 4, 5]
[Cat, Dog, Apple, Bag]
{3=C, 2=B, 1=A}
[]
{}
```

Private method in interface

Java 9 introduced private method in interface. Until java 8, you can add private default and static methods in interface, but from java 9 you can define normal private method in interface. Below is the example of private method that is being called in default method.

```
1. public interface TestInterface {
2.
3.    private void someUtilityMethod() {
4.
5.            System.out.println("I am private method");
6.    }
7.
8.    default void someDefaultMethod() {
9.            someUtilityMethod();
10.           }
11.
12. }
```

Java 11 Features

Java provides long term support (LTS) for java 11 after java 8 and the next long-term support is planned for java 17. Java 11 features are the combination of java 9, java 10, and java 11 features. Here we will talk about combination of java 10 and java 11 features.

Copyof(Collection)

Static method copyof was originally introduced in java 10. It provides unmodifiable copy of collection (List, Set, and Map). Below is the example.

```
1. List<String> words = new ArrayList<>();
2.
3. words.add("Bag");
4. words.add("Cat");
5.
6. List<String> wordsCopy = List.copyOf(words);
7.
8. words.add("Dog"); // modify words
```

180

```
9.
10.   System.out.println(words);
11.
12.   System.out.println(wordsCopy);
```

If you have created blank collection using of factory method that was introduced in java 9, now in java 11, you can copy collection into the blank collection. See the example below.

```
1.  List<String> words = new ArrayList<>();
2.  words.add("Bag");
3.  words.add("Cat");
4.
5.  List<String> emptyList = List.of();
6.
7.  emptyList = List.copyOf(words);
8.
9.  System.out.println(emptyList);
```

Output:
```
[Bag, Cat]
```

New String Methods

Java 11 introduced few new String utility methods, below are the details.

isBlank():
This method returns boolean value based on if String variable is empty or not. String containing only space is counted as empty string.

```
1.  System.out.println("   ".isBlank()); //true
2.
3.  System.out.println(" Hello ".isBlank()); //false
4.
5.  System.out.println("".isBlank()); //true
```

lines():

This static method returns a stream of string which is extracted from multi line string separated by a line terminator. A line terminator could be a new line (\n) or carriage return (\r). Below is the example.

```
1.  String str = "Hello\nDear\rHi";
2.  System.out.println(str);
3.  System.out.println(str.lines().collect(Collectors.toList())
    );
```

Output:
```
Hello
Dear
Hi
[Hello, Dear, Hi]
```

strip():

Java 11 introduces strip method to remove leading and trailing white space from string. Trim method of string was not Unicode aware and was not able to remove all kind of white spaces, but strip is Unicode aware and is able to remove all kind of white space. There are three version of strip, strip(), stripLeading(), and stripTrailing(). Strip remove white space from both the side of string, stripLeading removes all the leading whitespace from string, and stripTrailing removes all the trailing whitespaces from string. Below is the example.

```
1.  String str1 = " B ";
2.
3.  System.out.println("A" + str1.strip() + "C"); //ABC
4.
5.  System.out.println("A" + str1.stripLeading() + "C"); //AB C
6.
7.  System.out.println("A"+ str1.stripTrailing() + "C"); //A BC
```

Output:
```
ABC
AB C
A BC
```

repeat(int count):

Java 11 introduced new method repeat that take integer as an argument and returns string that is being repeated count number of times. The integer argument tells how many times the string will be repeated. Below is the example.

```
1.  System.out.println("A".repeat(5));
```

```
2. System.out.println("=".repeat(10));
```

Output:
AAAAA
===========

Nested class access control

In java 11 the inner class can access private variable and method from the outer class.
Below is the example.

```
1. public class Outer {
2.
3.    private static String str = "Hello";
4.
5.    static class Inner{
6.
7.            public static void print() {
8.                    System.out.println(str);
9.            }
10.           }
11.
12.           public static void main(String[] args) {
13.                   Outer.Inner.print();
14.           }
15. }
```

Output:
Hello

CI/CD

Continuous Integration (CI) and Continuous Delivery (CD) is the process of product development and release cycle. Continuous means ongoing. Integration and delivery is the ongoing process in CI/CD model. If Integration is not continuous then after certain time of development integration of code will become complex and it will take lots of time to resolve the integration issue and product required to tested again after resolving the integration issues.

To implement CI/CD you need to created deployment pipeline where integration and delivery happens continuously.
Below are the advantage of CI/CD.

- Speed of innovation: Speed of delivery and deployment will create fast feedback loop. You will get continuous feedback of your application and that will increase speed of innovation for your business.
- Fix issues early: The code will get integrated and tested continuously. Any issue related to your code will be identified and fixed continuously.

Continuous Integration

Once developer write the code and then validate and merge the code to the branch, the continuous integration quickly validates these changes. Continuous integration includes unit test execution and static code analysis. All unit test case should pass and if any code coverage policy is defined, it should satisfy the code coverage policy. For example, continuous integration will be successful only of code coverage is more than 80%. For static code analysis the policy may be defined as if there is no severe vulnerability found by SonarQube then it should pass continuous integration pipeline. If continuous integration fails, developer receives the notification and usually it fails code merge. Developer has to fix it and merge the code again to the specified branch.

Continuous Delivery

Continuous delivery pipeline starts after continuous integration is successful. Continuous delivery creates version of code in repository (git). The code changes went through Continuous Integration (CI), once successful the rest of the pipeline runs for Continuous Delivery (CD). In CD process it creates the jar/war and stores in antifactory as well as get it deployed in test environment. Continuous Delivery makes the code ready for one click deployment in production. Continuous delivery enables to code for continuous testing. Once jr/war deployed to the test environment functional test runs and check if functionality is working fine after code changes.

Continuous Deployment

Continuous Deployment is the process to deployment of code that went through the CI and CD pipeline successfully. This code is already tested in test environment. Blue-Green testing and deployment is the part of continuous deployment. Your deployment strategy could be Blue-Green deployment, Canary testing and deployment, Feature toggles, and Dark Launch.

www.ingramcontent.com/pod-product-compliance
Lightning Source LLC
Chambersburg PA
CBHW060133060326
40690CB00018B/3857